INSTANT POT COOKBOOK

Easy & Healthy Instant Pot Recipes For The Everyday Home – Delicious Triple-Tested, Family-Approved Pressure Cooker Recipes

© **Copyright 2017 - All rights reserved.**

The contents of this book may not be reproduced, duplicated or transmitted without direct written permission from the author.

Under no circumstances will any legal responsibility or blame be held against the publisher for any reparation, damages, or monetary loss due to the information herein, either directly or indirectly.

Legal Notice:
This book is copyright protected. This is only for personal use. You cannot amend, distribute, sell, use, quote or paraphrase any part or the content within this book without the consent of the author.

Disclaimer Notice:
Please note the information contained within this document is for educational and entertainment purposes only. Every attempt has been made to provide accurate, up to date and reliable complete information. No warranties of any kind are expressed or implied. Readers acknowledge that the author is not engaging in the rendering of legal, financial, medical or professional advice. The content of this book has been derived from various sources. Please consult a licensed professional before attempting any techniques outlined in this book.

By reading this document, the reader agrees that under no circumstances are is the author responsible for any losses, direct or indirect, which are incurred as a result of the use of information contained within this document, including, but not limited to, —errors, omissions, or inaccuracies.

Table of Contents

Introduction 1

Chapter 1: All About The Instant Pot 3

Chapter 2: Reasons For Buying The Instant Pot and Benefits 11

Chapter 3: How To Use The Instant Pot 17

Chapter 4: Freezer Cooking and The Instant Pot 25

Chapter 5: Safety Features 27

Conversion Charts 30

Chapter 6: Instant Pot Breakfast Recipes 33
    Oatmeal Apple Crisp 33
    Lemon Blueberry Steel Cut Oats 34
    German Chocolate Oatmeal 35
    Carrot Cake and Zucchini Bread Oatmeal 36
    Mushroom Thyme Oatmeal 37
    Quinoa Veggie Porridge 38
    Savory Porridge 39
    Breakfast Sandwiches 40
    Creamy Cheesy Grits 41
    Chocolate Chip French Toast 42
    Breakfast Burrito 43
    Cheesy Egg Bake 44
    Zucchini and Sweet potato Frittata 45
    Vegan Quiche 46
    Mushroom and Egg Breakfast 47
    Crustless Quiche 48
    Mexican Breakfast Casserole 49
    Vegetable Omelet 50
    Breakfast Hash 51
    Huevos Rancheros 52

INSTANT POT COOKBOOK

Chapter 7: Instant Pot Sauce Recipes 53
   Fresh Tomato Sauce 53
   Meaty Italian Spaghetti Sauce 54
   All-purpose Barbeque Sauce 55
   Marinara Sauce 56
   Eggplant Sauce 57
   Tomato Basil Sauce 58
   Ragu (Meat Sauce) 59
   Coffee Barbeque Sauce 60
   Chunky Pork and Mushroom Spaghetti Sauce 61
   Sweet Spaghetti Sauce 62
   Coney Island Hot Dog Sauce 63
   Italian Tomato Sauce 64
   Tabasco Sauce 65
   Sriracha Sauce 66
   Smoky Mustard Barbeque Sauce 67
   Pizza Sauce 68
   Bolognese Sauce 69

Chapter 8: Instant Pot Soups & Stews 71
   Creamy Chicken and Mushroom Soup 71
   Chicken and Vegetable Soup 72
   Spanish Sardines and Tomatoes Soup 73
   Creamy Crab Soup 74
   Hamburger Vegetable Soup 75
   Beef Potato and Quinoa Soup 76
   Pork Cabbage Soup 77
   Savory Cheese Soup 78
   Colombian Vegetable Soup 79
   Pumpkin and Corn Soup 80
   Cream of Zucchini Soup 81
   Vegetable Soup 82
   Simple Hamburger Stew 83
   Meatball Stew 84
   Lemony Garlic Lamb Stew 85
   German Style Pork Stew 86
   Seafood Stew 87
   Vegetarian Stew 88
   Easy Chili 89
   Vegetarian Chili 90

INSTANT POT COOKBOOK

Chapter 9: Instant Pot Snack Recipes 91
    BBQ Chicken Drummies 91
    Honey Garlic Chicken Wings 92
    Chicken Paprika 93
    Sweet n Spicy Meatballs 94
    BBQ Ribs 95
    BBQ Smoked Sausage 96
    Chinese Boiled Peanuts 97
    Meatballs 98
    Steamed Corn 99
    Loaded Potato Skins 100
    Dhokla 101
    Caponatina 102
    Pressure Cooked Red Potatoes 103
    Hummus 104
    Spicy Sweet Potatoes 105
    Asian Sesame Carrots 106
    Garlic Potatoes 107
    Spicy Chickpeas 108
    Cheesy Mushrooms 109
    Root Medley 110

Chapter 10: Instant Pot Meat Recipes 111
    Spicy Drumsticks 111
    Slow Cooked Chicken 112
    Creamy Chicken and Mushroom Potpie 113
    Chicken Risotto 114
    Seasoned Chicken, Potatoes & Green Beans 115
    Chicken Paprikash 116
    Turkey Osso Buco 117
    Mediterranean Roast Turkey 118
    Korean Beef 119
    Thai Red Curry 120
    Beef Nachos 121
    American Meat Loaf 122
    Italian Beef 123
    Easter Sunday Pot Roast 124
    Ragu with Ground Sirloin 125
    Spaghetti Squash and Meatballs 126
    Portuguese Chorizo and Peppers 127
    Super Easy Country Style Ribs 128
    Mexican Posole 129
    Mushroom & Spinach Pasta 130

Pork Chop Casserole 131
Pork & Mushrooms 132
Garlic Butter Leg of Lamb 133
Lamb with Vegetables 134
Ground Lamb & Chickpeas 135

Chapter 11: Instant Pot Fish and Seafood Recipes 137
Mahi Mahi with Asparagus, Broccoli and Spinach 137
Thai Green Fish Curry 138
Lemon Pepper Tilapia with Asparagus 139
Crawfish Tails 140
Spicy Lemon Salmon 141
Mediterranean Tuna Noodles 142
Scalloped Potatoes with Salmon 143
Tuna Casserole 144
Fish with Orange and Ginger Sauce 145
Citrus Fish 146
Salmon Al Cartoccio 147
Octopus and Potatoes 148
Shrimp Fried Rice 149
Coconut Cilantro Curry Shrimp 150
Shrimp and Artichoke Barley Risotto 151
Cheese and Prawns 152
Seafood Alfredo 153
Garlic Shrimp & Vegetables 154
Slow Cooked Crab 155
Shrimp Arrabbiata 156

Chapter 12: Instant Pot Vegetarian Recipes 157
Enchilada Quinoa 157
Golden Squash, Pepper, and Tomato Gratin 158
Swiss Chard with Chickpeas and Couscous 159
Vegetable Curry with Tofu 160
Vegetable Succotash 161
Mixed Vegetable Curry 162
Multi-Grain Fried Rice 163
Fresh Vegetable Mélange 164
Peas Risotto 165
Lentils with Vegetables 166
Vegetable Biryani 167
Vegetarian Conjee 168
Asian Crunchy Noodle Salad Bowl 169
Vegan Veggie Crumbs Casserole 170

Spinach & Corn Au Gratin 171
Vegetable Lasagna 172
Broccoli and Rice Casserole 173
Paneer Tikka Masala 174
Enchilada Orzo 175
Tofu Salad 176
Shepherd's Pie 177
Spinach Tortillas 178
Creamy Mushroom Polenta 179
Daal Maakhni 180
Vegetarian Tacos 181

Chapter 13: Instant pot Dessert Recipes 183
Peanut Butter Chocolate Cheesecake 183
Mini Salted Caramel Mocha Cheesecakes 184
Chocolate Fudge 185
Cherry Dump Cake 186
Mango Coconut Rice Pudding 187
Strawberry Pudding 188
Chocolate Peppermint Pudding 189
Mixed Berry Pudding 190
Pumpkin Custard 191
Spiced Apple Crunch 192
French Orange Crème 193
Flan with Caramelized Almonds 194
Crème Brulee 196
Caramel Custard 197
Stuffed Peaches 198
Apricot Crisp 199
Chocolate Covered Pretzel Rods 200
Sugared Walnuts 201
Calabash Halwa 202
Blackberry Grunt 203
Berry Compote 204
Caramel Fondue 205

Conclusion 207

Introduction

Do you want to be able to whip up tasty food without having to spend hours in the kitchen? Well, then the Instant Pot is the perfect appliance for you; in addition to saving you time and effort, it is quite handy and very simple to use and can definitely improve your overall health. The magic behind how this all works is in the use of pressured steam; through using this method, one is able to seal most of the nutrients in the cooked meal. The Instant Pot is a multi-programmed 3rd generation electric pressure cooker that performs all the functions that can be done by an electric pressure cooker, a slow cooker, rice cooker, a steamer, a yogurt maker, a sautéing pan, and a warming pot. If you want to own all of these appliances, but don't have the space to store it all, then an Instant Pot is a good investment.

In this book, you will find all the basic information that you will need about an Instant Pot for getting started. You will find information about the features of an Instant Pot, its various uses, benefits, safety precautions, tips on using the Instant Pot, and of course, loads of recipes as well. The conversion chart that has been provided in this book will help you in measuring out the required ingredients for the recipes given so that it doesn't cause any confusion. For everyone who values quick and convenient cooking, this appliance is indeed a blessing. You will just have to "set it" and then forget about it till your food is ready.

The recipes given in this book are easy to follow, healthy and simply delicious. All the recipes have been divided into different categories for the reader's convenience. As you master the recipes, feel free to make adjustments to them and customize them to your liking.

So, what are we waiting for? Let's get started.

CHAPTER 1

All About The Instant Pot

Let us learn a little about the Instant Pot before trying out all the different recipes that have been given in this book.

Pressure-cooking is the technique of cooking that makes use of a sealed container that doesn't allow any vapor to escape below a predetermined level of pressure. This causes the heating point of the water to rise and increases the pressure that's present in the vessel, and the pressure that's built up within the cooker allows the liquid in the cooking vessel to rise to an even higher temperature before it starts cooking. Denis Papin, a French Physicist, is credited with the invention of the pressure cooker in the year 1679. Papin was recognized for his studies in steam, and he invented a steam digester that would help in reducing the cooking time. The airtight cooker allowed him to make use of steam pressure for raising the boiling point of water and this enabled him to cook food quickly. Unfortunately, it didn't gain much recognition until a few centuries later; in fact, it was only at the time of World War II that the pressure cooker became a regular household kitchen appliance. When people began to realize the amount of fuel that can be saved, the ease with which a meal can be cooked, coupled with the shorter duration of cooking time, the pressure cookers popularity soared.

The simple pressure cookers were designed in a manner so that they can be used over a stovetop. For protecting the cooker against the dangers of overheating and exploding, there are various features like a regulator for steam, a safety valve mechanism, and an interlock mechanism that is pressure-activated. When the pressure within the cooker reaches a preset limit, then the regulator is pressed to one side due to this pressure build up, and it allows the excess of steam to escape. The piercing and troubling noise that you hear when the pressure is building up from a traditional stovetop cooker is due to the same reason.

The electric pressure cooker was invented sometime in the last decade, and it was indeed is a resourceful invention. The historians are still not sure about the inventor and the precise time of this invention but it's well noted that Mr. Yong Guang Wang, a Chinese scientist, filed the first patent for electric pressure cooker in the year 1991. At present, a pressure cooker manufacturer known as Midea Group owns this exclusive right.

The electric pressure cooker is made up of a vessel for pressure-cooking, and it is primarily made up of the cooking pot, the heating constituent, and sensors to detect temperature or pressure. The heating process in this is monitored by microprocessors that are built into the body and helps in reading and controlling the different sensors. This entire process results in something that is referred to as the formation of a closed-loop control system in technical terms. This system is comparable to the automatic cruise control system which most cars tends to make use of nowadays. The user just has to toss all the items into the cooking pot and simply then adjust the duration and settings of the pressure cooker depending upon the kind of food that is being cooked, and the pressure cooker will do the rest of the work. Overtime, the electronic pressure cookers have been developed further and now include a variety of cooking profiles like simmering, steaming, slow cooking, braising, and so on, by making use of different combinations as well as cooking temperatures, the time taken, and the pressure required. These developments resulted in the development of the new 3rd generation electric pressure cookers, the Instant Pot.

How does an Instant Pot work?

Three main parts constitute an Instant Pot. The first part is the lid, the second one is the inner pot, and the third part is housing. The two main features of the housing that you should be aware of are the safety valves that are present in them and the control panel. Let us take a closer look at the different parts of an Instant Pot.

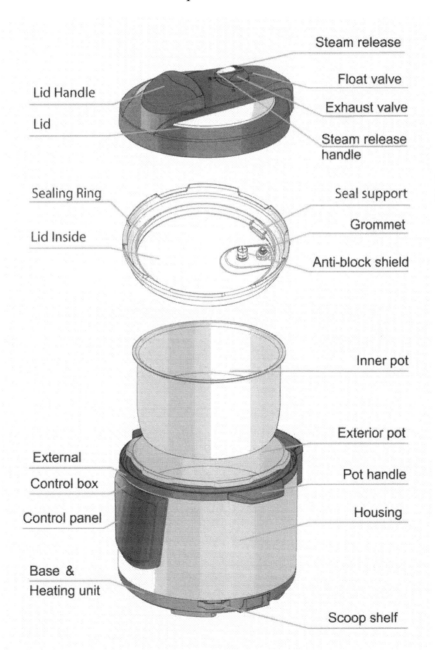

Inner Pot

The first part is the inner pot. This cooking pot is a detachable one, and it is present in the pressure cooker. This cooking pot is made of a mirror-polished stainless steel, which doesn't rust and also doesn't stick too much to food. This high quality grade of stainless steel is quite sturdy and has a copper coating on the bottom for providing uniform heating. The dimensions of the inner pot determine the capacity of the housing and to some degree the cost of the cooker as well. The capacity of this part can range from anywhere between 5 to 8 quarts.

Lid

The lid comes along with a gasket that acts as a sealing ring. The lid and the inner pot form an airtight space when the lid is secured on the cooker in a sealed position. This facilitates the increase of pressure within the pot when the amount of heat supplied to the inner pot increases. In some electric pressure cookers, if the lid hasn't been locked tightly into position, then opening it would create an unsafe operating condition because of all the pressure that is generated within the cooker. To prevent the cooker lids from being opened accidentally, electric pressure cookers come along with a pin-lock system, known as the float valve in the Instant Pot, which helps in preventing such situations. The pin essentially functions like a ballcock. Depending upon the pressure within the inner pot, the float valve is pushed upwards when the pressure increases to release steam. Once this has been pushed up, then the pin of the valve acts as a lock, and it stops the lid from moving from its place, even when the force increases. The Instant Pot also has a secondary power switch that is an added safety feature. If the lid has not been secured in the lock position, then the control mechanism of this appliance can detect this condition and will not let the user turn it on for heating.

Safety Valves

Akin to a regular pressure cooker, the pin of the float valve that has been mentioned above can be damaged due to excessive pressure or even temperature. Sans the pin, the float valve becomes a hole for the pressure to escape, and the pressure that's within the compartment will be released through this hole. If that's the case, then the float valve and the lid will have to be replaced for the safe operation of this appliance.

All the latest electronic pressure cookers make use of other safety assurances before they require any replacement of the parts. The Instant Pot in this case makes use of a patented innovation that helps in getting rid of any unwarranted pressure, even in the highly unlikely case of the ballcock pin being damaged. Usually, the only situation in which the built-up pressure can break out the inner pot is through the valve that's present on the top and is referred to as the pressure expulsion or the regulator valve. The pressure expulsion valve has got several anti-block shields that are present inside the lid and is designed in such a manner that under the usual operating range of pressure, it does not release any pressure when it is in a sealed arrangement. If the pressure goes beyond the operating range that is considered to be safe, the pressure release valve will be pushed upwards and similar to the workings of a conventional pressure cooker, the extreme pressure that is built up within the chamber will be released. The main difference lies in the workings of the pressure release valve that kicks in only when there is an excessive build-up of pressure.

Housing unit

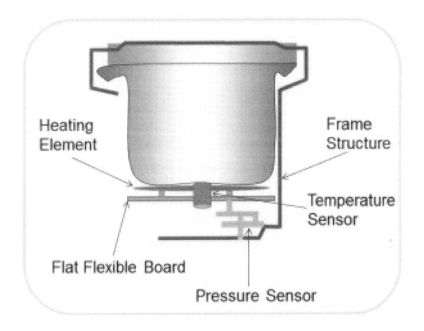

The Instant Pot has a heating component, a control box, and sensors for reading both pressure and temperature. This control box acts as the functioning and regulating part of the electronic pressure cooker. From the sensors, it monitors the warmth and the pressure that is building up within the inner pot. It has been outfitted with a microprocessor that helps in controlling functions like heating, timing, and even the complex cooking functions for which it's been programmed. This positive feedback system helps in creating perfect cooking conditions. An audible alarm will be sounded when the microprocessors detect an insecure operating situation and in even more serious situations, the power supply itself can be cut off.

The control box, which has a user interface allows for the activation of the preprogrammed cooking cycles for the different operations through the single key operation buttons. For instance, corn, peas, cauliflower, broccoli, and the like can be steamed in a less than a minute using the steam function.

Intelligent Pressure Cooking

Electronic pressure cookers usually operate within a pressure range of about 70kPa-80 kPa (Kilopascal) or about 10.15psi to 11.6 psi (Pound force per square inch). This means that they function within the temperature range of 115°C to 117°C or 239°F to 246°F. The initial pressure at the beginning of the cooking process can reach up to 105kPa or 15.2 psi, due to the delay in the dissipation of the heat. This is similar to the normal pressure cooker that reaches up to 15 psi, and then the heat gets eventually turned down.

By switching the heating element on or off, and also due to the variation in the heating intensity of the different temperatures and pressures, the optimal cooking result can be attained in a smarter way. Some of the electric pressure cookers, as the Instant Pot have certain intelligent cooking capabilities that can help you in achieving the best results. It can automatically alter the time for cooking and pressure required based on the type of food that you have chosen. The cooking period is also adjusted based on the quantity of food that's present within the cooker and also by measuring the preheating duration.

Three Generations of Electric Pressure Cookers

The electric pressure cookers have come a long way since the patent for it was filed for the first time on the 9th of January in the year 1991. Based on their capability of controlling the cooking process, they have been classified into three categories or generations.

1st Generation

The first generations of electric pressure cookers were fitted with a mechanical timer. These cookers have already been fitted with the essential sensors for detecting changes in pressure and temperature and act a moderator of the threshold limit. If either of the thresholds has been reached, then the power supply to the heating element is cut off. The only control that is accessible to the user is the mechanical cooking-time controller, which helps in getting an estimate of the cooking duration. The basic safety features and mechanisms like the locking of the lid under pressure, and excess-pressure protection valves have also already been implemented in these cookers. The electric pressure cookers that belong to the 1st generation are rarely seen in North America but are still quite popular in the Asian countries.

2nd Generation
The Second Generation Electric Pressure Cookers make use of digital controllers. These cookers are an improvement over the capability of the 1st generation ones due to this unique addition. Delayed Cooking is possible due to this improvement. The pressure sensor has also been connected to the controller electronically, and this means that a countdown timer can be displayed when the working pressure has been reached in the inner pot. The safety features have been further enhanced with the addition of different sensors. The most notable of all these are the improvement made to the lid. If the lid hasn't been fully locked, then the pressure-cooking will not start. This prevents the potential risk of the lid blowing up due to the buildup of pressure.

3rd Generation
The Third Generation Electronic Pressure Cookers are fitted with smart programming and have enhanced security features as well. The pressure and temperature sensors are quite advanced in this range of electronic pressure cookers, and they have sophisticated control mechanisms, thanks to the advancement in digital technology. These two features help in improving cooking results and also in maintaining consistency while enhancing safety. Each of these electric pressure cookers has been fitted with a microprocessor. The accurate readings from the pressure and the temperature sensors, along with the microprocessors can be programmed for performing different cooking tasks and techniques as well. The Smart Programs are fitted for specific cooking purposes by simply varying the intensities of the heat, temperature, pressure, and the time required. This helps in achieving efficient cooking that is consistent. A simple example would be the multigrain-cooking program that has been preset, and in this mode, the grains are soaked at 60-degree Celsius or 86-degree Fahrenheit before the actual cooking process starts.

With the advancement in the microprocessor programs, the scope of safety and sophistication has been widened as well. For instance, one common mistake that many make is misplacing the steam release at the open position at the begging of the cooking process. If the steam release is open, then there won't be any steam buildup. Irrespective of this, the earlier generations of cookers would continue the heating process, and if this situation isn't corrected in due course of the cooking, all the liquid that is present in the cooking pot would simply evaporate and ruin the meal. The 3rd Generation cooker comes with a built-in mechanism that is referred to as the Leaky Lid Protection, where the microprocessors help in detecting any excess pre-heating pressure leaks, and would stop the heating period with an alarm if there was.

Well, you might be wondering why it is important to know about the different electric pressure cooker models. The answer is simple; all the Instant Pot models are the 3rd generation electric pressure cookers!

CHAPTER 2

Reasons For Buying The Instant Pot And Benefits

Buying an Instant Pot is quite a good investment; don't worry about the price, it is totally worth it. If you feel that the Instant Pot that you have purchased isn't worth the expenditure that you have incurred, then you need to think again. After going through all the reasons that have been mentioned in this chapter, you will change your mind. In fact, the number of functions this appliance can perform will stun you.

Cook Beans Super Fast

This might pique your interest; you can cook beans in less than an hour. Soaked beans can be cooked in 15 to 20 minutes, and dry beans can be cooked within 35 to 40 minutes. Cooking beans has never been this easy. It normally takes several hours for slow cooking beans. Now, you might be concerned that this is a single use appliance and might not be fully won over, yet. If so, you will need to keep reading through all the points that are been mentioned in this chapter. Also, don't forget to try out the various bean-based recipes that have been mentioned in this book. You will appreciate the simplified process.

Make Perfect Brown Rice

Cooking rice sounds simple, doesn't it? Rice isn't easy to cook and to cook it to perfection can be quite challenging. The grain to water ratio that should be made use of in the case of brown rice is 1 to 1.25 and for white rice it's 1 to 1.5. It might seem like a lot lesser water than what you are used to. Well, you won't get crunchy rice. Instead, you will get perfect rice every single time. Instant Pot is about cooking food to perfection on a consistent basis. You can enjoy perfectly sticky and non-crunchy rice from now on. Different Instant Pot recipes have been mentioned in this book that you can make use of for cooking different rice-based dishes.

Steam/Cook Veggies in Minutes

What usually occurs is once you start cooking, you might walk away for a few minutes or start doing some other chore and forget about what you are cooking. Then, once you smell the food aroma cooking, you go running to check up on your dish. Everyone might have burnt his or her fare share of dishes without intending to do so. Vegetables are probably the most overcooked of the lot. Instant Pot makes life so much easier. Vegetables can be steamed or cooked within a few minutes, and the great thing is that, the cooking will stop when you programmed it too as well!

Built in Timer
With a crock-pot, you can leave the ingredients in it and then come back to fully cooked meals. Well, the Instant Pot is a step ahead of a Crock-pot. It has a built in timer that won't start cooking till you want it to. You needn't cook dinner in the morning itself. You can simply program it to start cooking at 4:30 pm and then keep it warm until the time that you get home. Even if you are at home, think about all the time that you are saving by setting it all up in advance and then not having to think about it until its actually time to have dinner.

Easy Clean Up
Cleaning might not be an engaging task, and it is quite a chore. Wouldn't you outsource it, if you could? You might avoid cooking a particular meal because of the cleaning that you will have to do once the meal is cooked. The Instant Pot is quite easy to clean. It comes with a removable stainless steel pot and a lid along with it. Those two things are the only things that you will have to wash.

Pressure Cooking Retains More Nutrients
Pressure-cooking helps in retaining more nutrients than any other form of cooking ever will. The short duration for which the food is cooked along with the little water that's used makes sure that all the nutrients are sealed in the food. The high pressure in the Instant Pot helps in making sure that the food is more digestible as well.

They are safe
You might have heard all the crazy stories about pressure cookers blowing up and that they are not safe. Well, don't let this scare you. The Instant Pot is 100% safe. It has various safety features that ensure that human error wouldn't cause any accidents. There are different built in safety features for controlling the pressure, temperature, and making sure the lid is locked. You will find more information about the safety features in the coming chapters.

Slow Cooker
The Instant Pot is almost the same size as a slow cooker, and it does the job of a slow cooker with just the push of a button. If you want to make use of your Instant Pot as a

slow cooker on a regular basis, then make sure that you are purchasing the optional lid along with it as well.

Sauté feature
The Instant Pot can also help you in sautéing by simply pressing a button. If you want to, you can toss in onions and garlic, then select the sauté option and get your other ingredients ready till the ones in the Pot are done being sautéed. Once all your other ingredients are ready, then you can add them to the pot and select any preprogrammed option, like Soup perhaps or anything else that you please.

Pressure-cooking has got several advantages in saving time and energy, preserving the nutrients in the food and eliminating all the harmful microorganisms that might be present in the food. Let us take a look at all the different benefits of cooking with an Instant Pot.

Saving Time & Energy
Food can be cooked much faster by pressure-cooking than by any other method of cooking. An Instant Pot can help you in reducing your cooking time by 70% when compared to the other methods of cooking. Since much less water is used and it is cooked in a fully insulated pot, much less, energy is required as well when compared to any other cooking technique like boiling or steaming while cooking on a stovetop. An Instant Pot will help you in saving energy when compared to a microwave as well.

Preserving Nutrients & Cooking Tasty Food
Pressure-cooking will help in ensuring that the heat is spread evenly and quickly. You do not need to immerse your food in the water, but there needs to be sufficient water to ensure that there is enough steam in the Pot. Because of this, all the nutrients in the food, like the different minerals and vitamins will stay intact in the food and won't dissipate. Steam will surround the food, and this means that air or exposure to heat won't oxidize the food. Therefore, fresh green foods will retain their color even after being cooked.

Food that is cooked in the Instant Pot is fully sealed so the water content and fresh juices within all the ingredients will stay in the Instant Pot and won't dissipate. This means that all the nutrients and flavors in the ingredients are trapped within the container and no steam or smell will spread throughout your home or your kitchen. This makes for a clean and an extremely convenient cooking environment. While you are steaming food in Instant Pot, you needn't make use of lots of water. You just need to add sufficient water to keep the cooker filled with pressure. This makes sure that all the vitamins and minerals within the food don't escape and aren't dissolved because of any water. Any cuts of meat can be cooked to perfection with this. If you are making use of any cut of meat that requires tenderizing and braising before it is fit for consumption, then this should be your go-to option. Meat with bone in it can be cooked to perfection. For instance, pork ribs can be cooked in it, and once the meat is succulently cooked, the bones would simply separate from the meat and the meat would become soft and tender. Pressure-cooking also allows whole grains and beans based meals to have a softer texture while keeping their flavor as well.

Another important feature of this appliance is that all the meals will be cooked consistently. This is possible because of the intelligent programming that makes sure that similar foods are cooked in a similar manner and also due to the even distribution of heat while cooking.

Intelligent Programming

The Instant Pot has got 12 operation buttons that will perform different cooking tasks like cooking rice, multigrain rice, sautéing, soup, poultry, meat and stew, chili and beans, steaming, slow cooking, keeping warm, and even for making yogurt. This one-button function will help you in achieving consistent results. For instance, take the "rice" button. While cooking rice, the Instant Pot will estimate the required amount of rice and water by measuring out the pre-heating time. The duration of the pressure keeping will vary depending upon this measurement and the stage of cooking. Each of these function buttons can be refined further by varying the range of the food from rare to well done, depending on your preferences.

Automatic Cooking

This is convenient and is an automated process. Each cook can be timed and then it would simply switch onto keeping the food warm once it is cooked. Unlike a conventional pressure cooker, you needn't stand and monitor the cooking time and process. Delayed Cooking is another fetching feature of the Instant Pot. This means that you can plan your meal well ahead of time. You needn't stand around and wait for your meal to be ready. This means that your cooking time is reduced by more than half. Wouldn't it be wonderful if you can come home to a freshly cooked meal and you don't even have to worry about doing a lot of dishes once you are done with the meal?

Clean & Pleasant

Conventional cookers have an image of these spitting and steaming monstrous pots that keep making rattling noises that can even scare an adult. The Instant Pot is quite the opposite of this. The Instant Pot is quiet and is fully sealed. This means that the pressure simply builds up in the inner pot and there is no chance of any steam escaping into the outer environment. Therefore, there won't be any smell spreading in your home or kitchen. Like mentioned earlier, this will help in trapping the flavors of the food within the container. Instant Pot will help you in cooking food without heating up the surroundings, and this would be well appreciated during summer time by reducing the electricity required for heating and cooling the food. The Instant Pot does help you in keeping your kitchen clean. There won't be any messy spills or splashes, and you don't have to clean up food that boils over. Everything is perfectly sealed and trapped within the inner pot. It is a kitchen-friendly appliance that requires minimal cleaning. It is a multipurpose appliance, and it will help you in getting rid of the clutter in your kitchen.

Eliminating Unsafe Micro-Organisms from Food

When the food gets cooked at high temperatures, which is above the boiling point of water, then this will help in killing all the harmful microorganisms that might be present in the ingredients like bacteria and viruses. The Instant Pot is a good way to sterilize your food; rice, wheat, corn, and even beans tend to carry different fungal poisons referred to as aflatoxins. These aflatoxins are produced by different species of fungi due to humid conditions and improper storage. Also, these are responsible for triggering a range of potent illnesses like liver cancer and might also play a role in hosting other triggers of cancer. Just heating the food to the boiling point of water does not necessarily destroy these harmful toxins. Cooking it at that temperature helps. Kidney beans are a very common ingredient and are mostly made use of for cooking chili. Well, these kidney beans have a particular toxin that's present in them, and the only way in which this can be destroyed is by cooking them at a high temperature for at least a period of ten minutes.

The Instant Pot is a versatile appliance indeed and will prove to be quite useful in your daily cooking.

CHAPTER 3

How To Use The Instant Pot

Six Simple Steps To Using Your Instant Pot

By this time, hopefully in front of you lies an Instant Pot and you are eager to utilize it to its full potential. It's very exciting as you unbox your Instant Pot and check out all the different functions available and it is even more exciting to understand how this equipment will improve your life.

The Instant Pot is easy to use and we will now commence with sharing the basics of how to use it in six simple steps.

1. **Determine The Duration Required**

   The first step is simple enough; simply understand how much time you will require to cook your meal. Although it's very simple in meaning, the difference it can make is enormous. A few minutes undercooked and the flavor isn't quite there, a few minutes overcooked and you'll be eating unappealing burnt crisps. In the recipe section are prepared meals with the time required to cook for perfection so hopefully you won't have an issue with this step.

2. **Ensure The Lid is Ready And Clean.**

For this step, there are 3 things to check.

a. Sealing ring is correctly fitted and sterile.
b. Float valve is free of food debris and easily moves up and down.
c. Steam release handle is clean and the longer part is pointing at the "Sealing" position.

Before cooking any meals, carefully check the above-mentioned steps to ensure the lid is ready for use.

3. **Place The Ingredients Into The Inner Pot**

   How difficult can it be to put ingredients into the inner pot? Well, it's not too difficult but there are just 2 points here to watch out for.

   a. If it could, position your meal into the center with it touching the edges of the inner pot.
   b. Use a trivet or a steamer basket if your meal requires it.

   These 2 extra steps are to safeguard your meal from becoming unevenly cooked.

4. **Plug Your Instant Pot To An Electrical Socket**

   A beeping sound will occur as your unit gets plugged in; this is step 4, you're almost there!

5. **Choose A Function**

   It's time for the fun part; using this all-in-one machine, you can make such a large combination of meals and it's exciting to learn the different functions! We'll go over each of the functions here for you and how to use them.

The control panel on an Instant Pot

FUNCTIONS

Soup

Default Time: 30 minutes
Adjust: 40 minutes or 20 minutes
Pressure Setting: High Pressure

Poultry

Default Time: 15 minutes
Adjust: 30 minutes or 5 minutes
Pressure Setting: High Pressure

Meat/Stew

Default Time: 35 minutes
Adjust: 45 minutes or 20 minutes
Pressure Setting: High Pressure

Bean/Chili

Default Time: 30 minutes
Adjust: 40 minutes or 25 minutes
Pressure Setting: High Pressure

Sauté

Used with lid off
Adjust: Less (Simmer), More (Brown)

Rice

Default Time: Automatically adjusts time duration depending on the ratio of water to rice.
Adjust: Non-adjustable
Pressure Setting: Low

Multi-grain

Default Time: 40 minutes
Adjust: 60 minutes or 20 minutes
Pressure Setting: High Pressure

Congee/Porridge
Default Time: 20 minutes
Adjust: 30 minutes or 15 minutes
Pressure Setting: High Pressure
Note: Don't perform the quick release for this function; otherwise the food may squirt from the pressure release valves.

Steam
Default Time: 10 minutes
Adjust: 15 minutes or 3 minutes
Pressure Setting: High Pressure
Note: Use a wire rack or steamer basket

Slow Cook
Default Time: 4 hours
Adjust: Low temperature or high temperature
Time Adjustments: Through utilizing the "+" and "-", you may adjust the cooking time

Yogurt
The Yogurt function in the Instant Pot is unique amongst electric pressure cookers and is another reason why people choose the Instant Pot.
There are a few steps in making Yogurt and we'll go over the essentials steps below.
1. Cleanse the inner pot.
2. Steps: Steam one cup of water for 1 minute.
3. Boil the milk

Steps: Simply press the "Yogurt" function and "adjust" until the screen displays "boil". Now we simply wait until this process is complete and the screen displays "Yogt."

4. Wait 25 minutes for the temperature to decrease.
5. Add live active cultures to the milk
6. Select the "Yogurt" function and let the default time of 8 hours run its course.

Manual
This function will allow you to choose your desired time. The maximum limit is 120 minutes. In the case that you have a certain time that isn't part of any "pre-set" functions, you can use this.

Adjust
This button allows you to change any of the "pre-set" functions to their adjustable settings.

Timer

This function allows you to delay the cook start time by a maximum limit of 24 hours. As an example, say you prepare your meal the night before and the cook time is 1 hour but you want it fresh when you get home at 5pm the next day. If you start it at 10pm, simply select a delay timer for 18 hours, that way it'll start at 4pm and be ready by 5pm.

Keep Warm

As a general rule, this feature should always be kept on, unless specific recipes call for it. What this does is keep your cooked meal warm for up to 10 hours in the event that you forgot or had to step out of the house.

6. Depressurizing Your Instant Pot

Once your meal is finished cooking, you'll have to get rid of the pressure in the Instant Pot. There are two methods to release the pressure.

a. Natural Release

To perform a natural release, all you have to do is turn off your Instant Pot and wait between 5 to 20 minutes depending on how much pressure is within the pot.

b. Quick Release

To perform a quick release, simply turn the steam release handle either to the left or right. An important note to make here is that when performing a quick release, use a towel or a cooking mitt; the hot steam that is released can cause serious burns, as it will be extremely hot.

Here are some general things to keep in mind when using the Instant Pot

1. The time settings must be pressed within 10 seconds of pressing the function key, after the 10-second mark, it is set.
2. When you hear the first beep, the food will enter into the pre-heat cycle.
3. Once it reaches the optimum pressure, you'll see steam coming out, for 30 seconds to 2 minutes so don't be alarmed.
4. There are 10 proven safety mechanism to prevent the Instant Pot from having the accidents that first generation pressure cookers had, so don't be worried, it's very safe.
5. Once the cook time is up, your Instant Pot will beep, then go into the "keep warm" mode, incase you are doing something else at the time, for up to 10 hours. Now

hopefully by this time, you are a proud owner of an Instant Pot and very excited to get cooking with it. The meals that take hours to cook can be cooked in minutes by making use of this appliance. Before stepping into the world of Instant Pot cooking, you might feel a little intimated and even slightly overwhelmed. You needn't worry. This isn't a scary pressure cooker like old stovetop models that seems like it's threatening to blow the whole place down every time it shakes menacingly. The Instant Pot is an innovative machine that is made of stainless steel and is highly sophisticated. This will indeed alter your cooking habits for sure. You probably have made use of a slow cooker and rice cooker in the past, but even then so, you will be blown away. Here are five tips that will help you in making the most of your Instant Pot.

Make use of the preset functions

For all those who are just getting started with the Instant Pot, familiarize yourself with all the different settings and take time to explore these options. You needn't worry about getting the time and the settings right, just chuck all the ingredients into the Instant Pot, select the preprogrammed setting stated in the recipes and simply wait for it work its magic. Once you are more at ease with the Instant Pot, you can start making adjustments to the time and temperature settings. The predetermined functions are the best way of getting started. You know, making chili might have been quite a tedious task in the past because it needs to be simmered on slow flame and watched carefully. Now, all that you need to do is toss all the ingredients into the Instant Pot, select the desired function and wait for about an hour, and voila, your chili is ready. You can pretty much cook anything you want using these preset functions. You can braise meat, cook your favorite curries, and serve delicious food with a fraction of the effort that usually goes in.

Reheat leftovers

At face value, the "Steam" option of the Instant Pot is meant to simply cook for a brief period. In addition, instead of using a microwave, you can make use of this function for reheating frozen food as well. You don't need to thaw the frozen food before placing it in the Instant Pot. Add a cup of water to the Instant Pot before you reheat, the moisture is important for increasing the pressure. For any packaged meals, you will simply have to remove the plastic wrap they come in and place the food on a steamer rack or trivet. For any frozen leftovers, you will simply have to place the food in a casserole dish (oven safe) and place it on the rack. The time taken will vary depending upon the quantity of the food that you are reheating; it can take anywhere between 3 to 10 minutes.

Sautéing

All the present Instant Pot models have a sauté; this is a feature that even a slow cooker doesn't have. Did you ever have to wash a pan or skillet after you have messily dumped ground meat or sautéed onions and garlic into your slow cooker, then you will understand why this preprogrammed, built in feature is amazing. The Instant Pot is a one-pot marvel, and you can make use of it as a stovetop skillet before switching over to the pressure cooker function. It is quite a flawless transition. All the recipes provided in this book are guaranteed to blow your mind.

Go bulk

You can cook as little or as much as you want with the Instant Pot. You can cook two servings of rice within 10 minutes, but you can also make use of it for whipping up large batches of food as well. The pressure power that the Instant Pot has got is quite amazing and will turn you into a good meal planner. You can simply cook more than the usual quantity of rice, beans, or any other building blocks of a basic meal and then store them in freezer safe bags. You will then simply have to defrost these precooked items, and you can toss together a quick and delicious meal in no time.

Keep it clean

One last tip, it might seem silly to remind you that you will need to wash the dishes, this one is really important. It is vital that the rubber sealing ring, as well as the anti-block shield that's inside the lid, are squeaky clean. The residue from all the pressure-cooked food can get accumulated in the rubber ring over a period of time, and this can lead to accumulation of odors as well. To ensure that your Instant Pot is in good working condition, you will have to remove these things and scrub them clean from time to time.

CHAPTER 4

Freezer Cooking and The Instant Pot

The one reason why people love cooking using an Instant Pot is its speed. You probably have cooked freezer meals in the past but it took you quite a long time; well, did you know that Instant Pots and cooking freezer meals are like the perfect match? Here is a list of the best Instant Pot tips for turning your freezer meals from your freezer into freshly warm meals.

Cooking food straightaway from its frozen condition! Therefore, this means that you can proceed to cook without having to go through the thawing step and still manage to get your freezer meal onto the dining table within no time. There is one little condition to this. Since the appliance is round, you shouldn't freeze your food in a flat bag. You get the concept, don't you? A square peg and a round hole, but you needn't worry. This doesn't throw a spanner in your works. The next tip will help you solve this problem.

You can freeze your meals in round plastic containers. Typically, you might be making use of the freezer-friendly bags and then you would lay them flat in the freezer to save space. Well, if you start freezing your meals in round plastic containers that can be directly popped into your Instant Pot. You can freeze them in 64-70 ounce containers. 64 ounces will give you four servings. This is the quantity that you would probably store in a freezer bag. Now you will have to place this freezer bag into containers, pans, pots, or something similar that can easily fit within your Instant Pot and then you can freeze them into that shape. This is a good option if you don't want to invest in new containers for your Instant Pot. You will just have to get creative. This works well for bigger pieces of non-veg that you might roast. Like whole chickens or rack of lamb. Also, placing the liquid components in another container and not just directly freezing them will prevent them from freezing up flat.

You should always allow your Instant Pot some additional time while you are cooking using frozen foods. You will still be able to get your meal on the table within no time, however, when you are cooking food that's frozen, it will take a while longer than a regular cook will. Since the food will have first to thaw and then cook in the appliance.

Make sure that you are careful while using dairy products or flour in the recipes. Dishes full of cheese, soups that contain cream, or even foods that are thickened by making use of flour aren't expressly forbidden from being cooked in the Instant Pot. However, you will have to carefully clean all the valves to make sure that no food is stuck in there. It is ideal to add these items at the sauté or the warming step of the preparation process.

If you are planning on frequently cooking in your Instant Pot, then you should make sure that you have purchased a separate insert made of stainless steel. This will also give you additional time to cook meals.

You should familiarize yourself with the different methods to release pressure so that you can make use of them. While making use of a pressure cooking setting, then the pressure within the Instant Pot will need to go someplace when the food preparation is all done. You can opt for a natural release, quick release, or a ten-minute natural release. If you want to make use of the pressure cooking function, then there needs to be some water in the Instant Pot.

CHAPTER 5

Safety Features

Most of the pressure cooker accidents that occurred in the past can be attributed the error committed on part of the user. The Instant Pot has been designed in such a fashion that it will help in getting rid of and avoiding most of the human error threats that plagued the former models. The Instant Pot has been developed by one of the top manufacturers of electric pressure cookers, and all the Instant Pots available for sale have been certified by UL/ULC.

The pressure cookers that were meant for stovetop usage make use of the weight of the pressure regulation that is on their lids for restricting the amount of cooking pressure that can get accumulated in the vessel. The patented pressure sensor technology that is made use of in an Instant Pot helps in regulating the pressure build up within the inner pot in a manner that is more precise and even automatic. When the pressure starts to build up within the inner pot of the vessel, the Flat Flexible Board shifts down, and this triggers the built-in pressure sensors. In a similar manner, when the pressure decreases in the cooker, the Flat Flexible Board moves upwards, and even this triggers the pressure sensors. The pressure sensor helps in controlling the amount of power and heating that should be maintained within the preset range present in the Instant Pot. The pressure sensor, like its name suggests, helps in maintaining the pressure build up in the Instant Pot to avoid any accidents. Apart from this ingenious safety feature, here are the ten safety features that are built into the Instant Pot.

Feature#1: Lid Close Detection
If the lid of the Instant Pot hasn't been closed properly, then the appliance will not be able to activate its function of pressurized cooking. If the lid if even partially open, the only functions that would work are the keep-warm and the sauté options.

Feature#2: Leaky Lid Protection

If the cooker lid has any leakage in it, the cooker will not be able to reach the optimum preset level of pressure. The leakage could be caused because of a variety of reasons such as if the stem release hasn't been properly closed, or perhaps if the sealing ring isn't fully sealed. If this function weren't enabled, then this could lead to the burning of your food. The Instant Pot helps in detecting this by taking note of the time taken for pre-heating. If the pre-heating process were taking longer than usual, then the programming would automatically switch the Instant Pot onto the Keep-warm feature for avoiding the food from getting burnt.

Feature#3: Lid Lock under Pressure

To prevent the accidental opening of the cooker, the lid will remain locked to make sure that the cooker is pressurized properly.

Feature#4: Anti-blockage Vent

It is very likely that during the cooking process, certain food particles could restrict the release of the steam by jamming the vent. The Instant Pot has a vent shield that has been specifically structured to avoid the jamming of the steam vent.

Feature#5: Automatic Temperature Control

The thermostat that is present under the inner pot of the Instant Pot helps in regulating the temperature of the inner pot and makes certain that it is within a safe range depending upon the type of food that is being cooked.

Feature#6: High-Temperature Warning

If the cooker is functioning without sufficient water or moisture, then there won't be sufficient pressure build up in the pot, and the cooking process would halt. The most likely outcome of this would be overheating. Excessive temperature might also occur due to different situations such as where the inner pot is missing, not in proper contact with the heating element of the cooker or perhaps the inner pot has got a heat-dissipating problem. The problem of heat dissipation in the inner pot can be caused if there is burnt starch at the lining of the inner pot that's blocking the heat. In such conditions, the Instant Pot will simply stop heating when the temperature has reached a certain limit.

Feature#7: Temperature and Power Protection

The Instant Pot has been equipped with a particular fuse that will disconnect itself when the power has reached a high temperature; that is anywhere between 169°C to 172°C or 336°F to 341.6°F or if there's an extremely high electrical current passing through. An unusually high electrical current if drawn by the cooker points out an unsafe condition.

Feature #8: Automatic Pressure Control
The Instant Pot comes with a patented pressure sensor mechanism that ensures that the operating pressure of this appliance doesn't exceed the range of 70kPa to 80kPa or 10.12psi to 11.6psi.

Feature#9: Pressure Regulator Protection
If the pressure in the Instant Pot goes beyond 105kPa or 15.23 psi, then the steam release will be pushed aside to allow for the excess steam to be pushed out of the inner pot and for lowering the excess pressure that has been building up in the pot. This is similar to the function of the pressure regulators that are present in a stovetop pressure cooker.

Feature#10: Excess Pressure Protection
If the pressure gets too high and this caused the pressure regulator protection that has been mentioned in the previous point to malfunction, then the internal protection mechanism present in the Instant Pot will be activated, and this shifts the inner pot downwards so that a gap is created between the lid and the inner pot. This will help in the release of steam from the internal chamber and stop the excessive heating.

Conversion Charts

US Liquid Volume Measurements	
Measure	**Equivalent**
8 Fluid ounces	1 Cup
1 Pint	2 Cups (16 fluid ounces)
1 Quart	2 Pints (4 Cups)
1 Gallon	4 Quarts (16 Cups)

US Dry Volume Measurements	
Measure	**Equivalent**
1/16 teaspoon	Dash
1/8 teaspoon	a pinch
3 teaspoons	1 Tablespoon
1/8 cup	2 tablespoons (= 1 standard coffee scoop)
1/4 cup	4 Tablespoons
1/3 cup	5 Tablespoons plus 1 teaspoon
1/2 cup	8 Tablespoons
3/4 cup	12 Tablespoons
1 cup	16 Tablespoons
1 Pound	16 ounces

US to Metric Conversions	
Measurements	Equivalent
1/5 teaspoon	1 ml (ml stands for milliliter, one thousandth of a liter)
1 teaspoon	5 ml
1 tablespoon	15 ml
1 fluid oz.	30 ml
1/5 cup	50 ml
1 cup	240 ml
2 cups (1 pint)	470 ml
4 cups (1 quart)	.95 liter
4 quarts (1 gal.)	3.8 liters
1 oz.	28 grams
1 pound	454 grams

CHAPTER 6

Instant Pot Breakfast Recipes

Oatmeal Apple Crisp

Servings: 6
Total time taken: 25 min

Ingredients:
- 6 cups apples, peeled, sliced
- 1 ½ cups quick cooking oats
- 1 ½ tablespoons lemon juice
- ¼ cup flour
- ¾ cup brown sugar
- ¼ cup margarine, melted
- 1 ½ teaspoons cinnamon
- ¾ teaspoon salt
- 2 ½ cups water

Directions:
1. Sprinkle lemon juice over the apples.
2. Mix together oats, flour, sugar, salt, margarine and cinnamon.
3. Take a greased tin or metal bowl that is smaller than the cooker and fits in the pot. Place a layer of apples. Next layer with the oats mixture. Repeat the layers and finally place apples in the topmost layer. Cover the tin with aluminum foil.
4. Switch on the instant pot and pour water in it.
5. Place a rack inside the pot and place bowl on the rack.
6. Close the lid and select the "Multi-grain" function and "Adjust" down to 20 minutes.
7. Quick release the pressure.
8. Serve warm.

Lemon Blueberry Steel Cut Oats

Servings: 4
Total time taken: 25

Ingredients:
- 2 cups steel cut oats
- 6 cups water
- 2 tablespoons lemon zest, grated
- 2 tablespoons butter
- 1 cup half and half
- 4 tablespoons sugar or sweetener of your choice to taste
- ½ teaspoon salt
- 2 cups blueberries, fresh or frozen
- ½ cup chia seeds

Directions:
1. Switch on the Instant Pot and select the "Sauté" option.
2. Add butter to the cooking pot. When the butter melts, add oats and stir well until the oats are lightly toasted.
3. Add water, half and half, sugar, salt and lemon zest and mix well. Close the lid of the pot.
4. Select the "Multi-grain" option and "Adjust" down to 20 minutes.
5. Quick release the remaining pressure.
6. Add blueberries and chia seeds. Mix well and remove the cooking pot. Set-aside until warm.
7. Serve with milk and some more maple syrup if you desire. Tastes great with sliced almonds.

German Chocolate Oatmeal

Servings: 4
Total time taken: 4 hrs. 10 min

Ingredients:
- 1 cup steel cut oats
- 1 cup light coconut milk
- 3 cups water
- 4 tablespoons brown sugar or to taste
- 2 tablespoons cocoa, unsweetened
- Shredded coconut, sweetened to serve
- ½ cup pecans to serve

Directions:
1. Switch on the Instant Pot.
2. Add all the ingredients into the inner pot and stir well.
3. Close the lid and lock the pot. Select "Slow Cook" option and use the default time of 4 hours.
4. Top with coconut and pecans and serve.

Carrot Cake and Zucchini Bread Oatmeal

Servings: 4
Total time taken: 3 hrs. 15 min

Ingredients:
- 1 small zucchini, peeled, grated
- 1 large carrot, peeled, grated
- 1 cup steel cut oats
- ½ cup pecans, chopped
- 1/8 teaspoon ground cloves
- 1/8 teaspoon ground nutmeg
- ¾ teaspoon ground cinnamon
- 2 teaspoons vanilla extract
- 3 cups vanilla flavored non-dairy milk
- 4 tablespoons agave nectar or maple syrup

Directions:
1. Switch on the Instant Pot.
2. Add all the ingredients into the cooking pot and stir well.
3. Close the lid and lock the pot. Select the "Slow Cook" option and set the timer for 3 hours.

Mushroom Thyme Oatmeal

Servings: 4-5

Total time taken: 25 min

Ingredients:
- 1 ½ cups steel cut oats
- 1 tablespoon olive oil
- 3 tablespoons butter
- 2 cups cremini mushrooms, sliced
- 4 cloves garlic, minced
- 1 large onion, chopped
- 5 sprigs fresh thyme + extra for garnishing
- 2 cups vegetable broth
- 1 cup water
- ¾ cup smoked gouda cheese, finely grated
- Salt to taste
- Pepper to taste

Directions:
1. Switch on the Instant Pot.
2. Add butter to the cooking pot.
3. Select the "Sauté" option. When the butter melts, add onions and sauté until translucent. Add garlic and sauté for about a minute until fragrant.
4. Add oats and sauté for a minute. Add broth, water, thyme, salt and pepper.
5. Press the "Cancel" Button.
6. Close the lid. Select the "Multi-grain" function and "Adjust" down to 20 minutes.
7. Let the steam release naturally for 10 minutes and then quick release excess steam. Transfer into a serving bowl.
8. Meanwhile, add mushrooms and select the "Sauté" function and cook until golden brown.
9. Add cheese and mushroom to the bowl and stir. Garnish with thyme and serve.

Quinoa Veggie Porridge

Servings: 2
Total time taken: 3 hrs. 10 min

Ingredients:
- ¼ cup quinoa, rinsed
- 1 stalk celery, chopped
- 1 onion, chopped
- 1 carrot, peeled, chopped
- ½ cup squash, chopped
- 2 green onions, sliced
- 1 small piece kombu sea vegetable
- Miso to serve

Directions:
1. Switch on the Instant Pot.
2. Add all the ingredients to the cooking pot and stir well.
3. Close the lid. Select the "Slow Cook" function and set the timer for 3 hours.
4. Add miso, stir and serve.

Savory Porridge

Servings: 4
Total time taken: 30 min

Ingredients:
- 1 cup bulgur
- 1 onion, chopped
- 2 tablespoons oil
- 1 large carrot, cubed
- ½ cup green peas
- 1 ½ teaspoon salt
- ½ teaspoon red chili flakes
- 2 tablespoons lemon juice
- 4 cups water

Directions:
1. Switch on the Instant Pot.
2. Select the "Sauté" function. Add oil and onions and sauté until translucent. Add bulgur and "Adjust" for more heat for 3-4 minutes.
3. Add the rest of the ingredients except lemon juice.
4. Close the lid and select the "Porridge" function and use the default time of 20 minutes.
5. Let a natural release occur for 15 minutes then open the lid.
6. Add lemon juice, stir and serve

Breakfast Sandwiches

Servings: 3
Total time taken: 15 min

Ingredients:
- 6 slices rye bread, toasted
- 3 eggs
- 3 thin slices prosciutto
- 3 tablespoons cheddar cheese, shredded
- Pepper powder to taste
- Salt to taste
- 3 cups water
- ½ teaspoon olive oil

Directions:
1. Switch on the Instant Pot.
2. Pour water into the cooking pot and place a streamer tray.
3. Sprinkle a couple drops of olive oil into 3 ramekins. Crack an egg into each of the ramekins.
4. Season with salt and pepper. Sprinkle cheddar cheese over it. Cover the ramekins with aluminum foil and place the ramekins on the steamer tray.
5. Close the lid and set the "Manual" option. Set the timer for 6 minutes. Let the pressure release naturally.
6. Remove the ramekins from the pot. Run a knife all around the edges and slowly remove the cooked eggs from the ramekins and invert on 3 toasted bread slices. Cover with the remaining 3 slices and your sandwiches are ready.

Creamy Cheesy Grits

Servings: 2-3
Total time taken: 30 min

Ingredients:
- ½ cup stone ground grits
- 1 cup half and half or milk
- 1 cup water
- 8 ounces cheddar cheese
- 2 tablespoons butter + extra to garnish
- 1 ½ cups water
- 2 tablespoons olive oil

Directions:
1. Switch on the Instant Pot.
2. Set the "Sauté" function. Add oil and grits and toast it lightly. Press Cancel button.
3. Add rest of the ingredients.
4. Close the lid. Select the "Manual" option and set timer for 10 minutes.
5. Let the pressure release naturally for 15 minutes and quick release excess pressure.

Chocolate Chip French Toast

Servings: 4
Total time taken: 4 hours 10 minutes

Ingredients:
- 6 cups French bread, cubed
- 1 cup milk
- 2 eggs
- 1 teaspoon vanilla extract
- 1/3 cup semi sweet chocolate chips
- 1/3 cup packed brown sugar
- 1 teaspoon ground cinnamon

Directions:
1. Grease the inside of the cooking pot with oil. Place bread at the bottom of the pot.
2. Whisk together eggs, milk, sugar, vanilla and cinnamon in a bowl and pour over the bread. Stir well.
3. Top with chocolate chips.
4. Switch on the Instant Pot.
5. Close the lid. Select the "Slow Cook" function and set the timer for 4 hours.

Breakfast Burrito

Servings: 3
Total time taken: 25 min

Ingredients:
- 1 ½ tablespoons olive oil
- 6 eggs, boiled, peeled, diced
- 1/3 cup tomatoes, diced
- 1 medium onion, diced
- 3 tablespoons fresh cilantro, chopped
- ¾ cup cooked black beans, warmed
- Salt to taste
- Pepper powder to taste
- 3 large tortillas, warmed according to the instructions on the package
- 1 medium avocado, peeled, pitted, diced
- 1/3 cup water
- 3 tablespoons sour cream (optional)
- 3 tablespoons cheddar cheese, shredded

Directions:
1. Switch on the Instant Pot and select the "Sauté" function.
2. Add olive oil. Sauté for a couple of minutes and add onions, tomatoes, cilantro, water and salt.
3. Close the lid. Select the "Poultry" function and "Adjust" down to 5 minutes.
4. When the timer goes off, release the pressure with quick release.
5. Place the tortillas on your work area. Divide the egg mixture among the tortillas. Divide the beans and place over the egg mixture. Place some avocado slices in the center.
6. Spread a tablespoon of sour cream. Sprinkle cheese. Roll and serve.

Cheesy Egg Bake

Servings: 6
Total time taken: 30 min

Ingredients:
- 12 eggs
- 9 slices bacon, chopped
- 1 cup mushrooms, sliced
- 1 red bell pepper, chopped
- 1 green bell pepper, chopped
- 1 yellow bell pepper, chopped
- 2 green onions, chopped
- 1 ½ cups cheddar cheese, shredded + extra to top
- 3 cups frozen hash browns
- 1/3 cup milk

Directions:
1. Select the "Sauté" function and add bacon. Cook until crisp. Add hash browns and sauté for a couple of minutes.
2. Whisk together in a bowl rest of the ingredients except green onions and pour into the pot.
3. Cover and select the "Poultry" option and "Adjust" down to 5 minutes.
4. Sprinkle green onions and cheese then serve.

Zucchini and Sweet potato Frittata

Servings: 6
Total time taken: 3 hrs. 20 min

Ingredients:
- 3 teaspoons ghee or coconut oil
- 12 eggs, whisked well
- 2 medium sweet potatoes, peeled, chopped into slices
- 3 tablespoons fresh parsley, chopped
- 3 medium zucchinis, sliced
- 1 small yellow bell pepper, sliced
- 1 small green bell pepper, sliced
- Salt to taste
- Pepper powder to taste
-

Directions:
1. Grease the inside of the cooking pot with melted ghee.
2. Place the sweet potatoes in the pot.
3. Next layer with zucchini followed with bell peppers.
4. Add salt and pepper to the whisked eggs and pour in the pot.
5. Switch on the Instant Pot.
6. Close the lid. Select the "Slow Cook" function and set the timer for 3 hours.
7. When done, garnish with parsley. Cut into wedges and serve.

Vegan Quiche

Servings: 4
Total time taken: 3 hrs. 15 min

Ingredients:
- 20 ounces frozen spinach, thawed, squeezed of excess moisture
- 1 cup onions, chopped
- 16 ounces mushrooms, sliced
- 28 ounces firm tofu, press to remove excess moisture
- 4 cloves garlic, minced
- 4 tablespoons nutritional yeast
- 1 teaspoon dried basil
- 1 teaspoon dried thyme
- ½ teaspoon pepper powder
- ½ teaspoon red pepper flakes
- Salt to taste
- 2 tablespoons olive oil
- 2 tablespoons apple cider vinegar
- 2 tablespoons lemon juice
- 2 teaspoons lemon zest, grated
- Cooking spray

Directions:
1. Spray the inside of the cooking pot with cooking spray.
2. Switch on the Instant Pot.
3. Select the "Sauté" function. Add oil, garlic, onions, spinach, and mushrooms.
4. Add salt, pepper, basil, and thyme, chili flakes. Sauté for a few seconds.
5. Blend together tofu, lemon zest and juice, and vinegar until smooth. Pour into the pot.
6. Add nutritional yeast and fold. Press the "Cancel" button.
7. Close the lid. Select the "Slow Cook" function and set the timer for 3 hours.
8. When done, cut into wedges and serve.

Mushroom and Egg Breakfast

Servings: 2
Total time taken: 20 min

Ingredients:
- 1 red onion, chopped
- 1 green bell pepper, chopped
- 2 tablespoons olive oil
- 2 garlic cloves, chopped
- 1 teaspoon chili flakes
- 1 cup portabella mushrooms, sliced
- 1 cup shiitake mushrooms, sliced
- 2 eggs, beaten
- Salt to taste
- Pepper to taste
- Cilantro to sprinkle
-

Directions:
1. Switch on the Instant Pot
2. Select the "Sauté" function. Add the oil, onions, and garlic to a pot and sauté until brown.
3. Add the chili flakes, bell pepper, mushrooms, salt and pepper and mix until well combined. Press the "Cancel" button.
4. Add eggs.
5. Cover and select the "Manual" option then set the timer for 5 minutes. Sprinkle cilantro and serve.

Crustless Quiche

Servings: 4
Total time taken: 60 min

Ingredients:
- 9 eggs, well beaten
- ¾ cup milk
- ¼ teaspoon pepper powder or to taste
- ½ teaspoon salt or to taste
- ¾ cup ham, diced
- 1 ½ cups ground sausage, cooked
- 6 slices bacon, cooked, crumbled
- 3 large green onions, sliced
- 1 ½ cups cheese, shredded

Directions:
1. Whisk together in a bowl, eggs, milk, salt and pepper.
2. Place bacon, sausage, ham, green onions and cheese in a soufflé dish. Mix well. Pour beaten egg mixture over it. Mix until well combined. Cover the dish with aluminum foil.
3. Place a metal trivet at the bottom of the cooking pot. Add 1-½ cups of water. Place the dish over the trivet.
4. Switch on the Instant Pot.
5. Close the lid and select the "bean/chili" option and use the default time of 30 minutes.
6. When the timer goes off, let the steam go off naturally for 10 minutes and then release the pressure with a quick release.
7. Remove the dish from the pot and discard the foil. If you like the top browned, then sprinkle some more cheese over it. Broil until the brown color you desire is achieved.
8. Serve immediately.

Mexican Breakfast Casserole

Servings: 6
Total time taken: 3 hrs. 15 min

Ingredients:
- 12 eggs
- 1 ½ pounds bulk chorizo, cooked, drained
- 2 ¼ cups milk
- 12 corn tortillas
- 1 large red bell pepper, chopped
- 2 jalapeños, deseeded, finely chopped
- 1 cup green onions, chopped
- 1 ½ cups chunky salsa
- 1 ½ cup pepper Jack cheese, shredded
- Salt and pepper to taste
- ¼ cup fresh cilantro

Directions:
1. Spray the cooking pot with cooking spray.
2. Whisk together in a bowl, eggs, salt, pepper and milk.
3. Retain about 2 tablespoons each of green onions and red bell peppers and ½ cup cheese and set the rest aside for layering.
4. Place 3 tortillas at the bottom of the Instant Pot. Place 1/3 the chorizo over it followed by 1/3 bell pepper, 1/3 red bell pepper and 1/3 the cheese.
5. Repeat the above step twice. Place the remaining 3 tortillas over it. Pour the egg mixture over it.
6. Switch on the Instant Pot.
7. Close the lid. Select the "Slow Cook" function and set the timer for 3 hours.
8. Garnish with cilantro, green onion, bell pepper, and cheese that were retained and serve with salsa.

Vegetable Omelet

Servings: 1
Total time taken: 20 min

Ingredients:
- 3 eggs
- ½ cup broccoli florets
- 1 clove garlic, minced
- ½ small yellow onion, chopped
- ½ red bell pepper, chopped
- A pinch chili powder
- Salt and pepper to taste
- A pinch garlic powder
- Chopped tomatoes, onions and parsley to top
- Grated cheese to top
- Cooking spray

Directions:
1. Whisk whites until fluffy. Add yolks and whisk again. Add vegetables and seasonings.
2. Spray the cooking pot with cooking spray. Pour eggs over it.
3. Switch on the Instant Pot.
4. Close the lid. Select the "Steam" function and use the default time of 10 minutes.
5. When done, carefully remove on to a plate and serve with toppings.

Breakfast Hash

Servings: 6
Total time taken: 20 min

Ingredients:
- 8-10 medium potatoes, peeled, shredded, squeeze the excess moisture in it
- 12 eggs, beaten
- 2 cups bacon, cooked, crumbled
- 2 cups cheese, grated
- ½ cup water
- Cooking spray

Directions:
1. Spray the inside of the cooking pot with cooking spray. Select the "Sauté" function and add potatoes and sauté until brown.
2. Add rest of the ingredients and stir.
3. Switch on the Instant Pot.
4. Close the lid. Select the "Steam" function and "Adjust" down to 3 minutes.
5. Stir and serve with toast.

Huevos Rancheros

Servings: 3
Total time taken: 30 min

Ingredients:
- 1 ½ cups prepared salsa
- 1 tablespoon butter, melted
- 6 eggs
- Salt to taste
- Pepper powder to taste
- A few tortillas or tortilla chips

Direction:
1. Divide the salsa amongst 6 ramekins.
2. Drizzle the melted butter all around the inner sides of the ramekins (above the salsa).
3. Crack an egg into each of the ramekins. Cover each ramekin with aluminum foil such that the water from the pot does not enter the ramekins.
4. Pour a cup of water to the cooking pot. Place the steamer rack inside the pot.
5. Place the ramekins on the steamer. Close the lid.
6. Select the "Congee/Porridge" function and "Adjust" down to 15 minutes.
7. When the cook time is over, allow 10 minutes for a natural release.
8. If you are using tortillas, warm the tortillas and serve the rancheros with the ramekins or just serve with tortilla chips.

CHAPTER 7

Instant Pot Sauce Recipes

Fresh Tomato Sauce

Servings: 4-6
Total time taken: 4 hrs. 15 min

Ingredients:
- 15 medium tomatoes, diced
- 6 cloves garlic, peeled, minced
- 2 medium carrots, diced
- 2 medium onions, diced
- 4 bay leaves
- 1 ½ cups broth
- 3 tablespoons olive oil
- 3 tablespoons Italian seasoning
- 3 teaspoons pepper powder
- 1 ½ tablespoons red pepper flakes
- 1 ½ teaspoons salt

Directions:
1. Add all the ingredients to the inner pot and stir well.
2. Switch on the Instant Pot.
3. Close the lid. Select the "Slow Cook" function and use the default time of 4 hours.
4. When cool enough to handle, blend until smooth.
5. Use as required. If you need to store it, then place in freezer safe containers and freeze.

Meaty Italian Spaghetti Sauce

Servings: 12
Total time taken: 4 hrs. 15 min

Ingredients:
- 1 cup onion, chopped
- 1 pound Italian pork sausage or ground beef
- 2 cloves garlic, finely chopped
- 1 cup fresh mushrooms, sliced
- 14 ounces canned diced tomatoes, with liquid
- ½ a 6 ounce can tomato paste
- 1 can (15 ounces) tomato sauce
- ½ tablespoon sugar
- 1 tablespoon dried basil leaves
- Salt to taste
- Pepper powder to taste
- 1 teaspoon dried oregano
- ½ teaspoon red pepper flakes

Directions:
1. Switch on the Instant Pot.
2. Select the "Sauté" function and press "Adjust" once for more heat.
3. Add onions, mushrooms, garlic and sausages and cook until pink. Press the "Cancel" button. Drain the excess fat.
4. Add the rest of the ingredients.
5. Close the lid. Select the "Slow Cook" function and use the default time of 4 hours.

All-purpose Barbeque Sauce

Servings: 6-8
Total time taken: 2 hrs. 5 min

Ingredients:
- ½ cup vinegar
- 2 cups ketchup
- 1 small onion, minced
- 2 tablespoons brown sugar
- 1 teaspoon hot pepper sauce
- 2 tablespoons Worcestershire sauce
- 2 cups water
- 2 teaspoons celery seeds
- Salt to taste

Directions:
1. Add all the ingredients to the inner pot.
2. Switch on the Instant Pot.
3. Close the lid. Select the "Slow Cook" function and set the timer for 3 hours.
4. Transfer into an airtight container and refrigerate until use.

Marinara Sauce

Servings: 10-12
Total time taken: 20 min

Ingredients:
- 3 cans (28 ounces each) crushed tomatoes
- ½ cup red lentils, rinsed
- 3 cups sweet potatoes, cubed
- 5 cloves garlic, minced
- 1 ½ teaspoons salt
- 2 ½ cups water

Directions:
1. Add all ingredients to the inner pot and stir well.
2. Switch on the Instant Pot.
3. Close the lid. Select the "Manual" option and set the timer for 13 minutes. Open the lid when the pressure releases naturally.
4. Stir and mash simultaneously and cool. Pour into a jar and refrigerate until use.

Eggplant Sauce

Servings: 12
Total time taken: 4 hrs. 15 min

Ingredients:
- 2 pounds eggplant, cut into 1 inch cubes
- 4 cloves garlic, chopped
- 1 large onion, chopped
- 4 cans (14 ½ ounce each) diced tomatoes
- 2 cans (6 ounce each) Italian tomato paste
- 8 ounces mushrooms, sliced
- ½ cup water
- ½ cup dry red wine
- 3 teaspoons dried oregano
- Pepper powder to taste
- Salt to taste

Directions:
1. Add all the ingredients into the inner pot.
2. Switch on the Instant Pot.
3. Close the lid. Select the "Slow Cook" option and use the default time of 4 hours.
4. Serve over pasta garnished with olives, parsley and cheese.

Tomato Basil Sauce

Servings: 6-8
Total time taken: 20 min

Ingredients:
- 2 ½ pounds Roma tomatoes, chopped
- 1 onion, chopped
- 4 cloves garlic, minced
- 2 tablespoons olive oil
- 1 teaspoon garlic powder
- 1 bay leaf
- 1 teaspoon salt
- 1 teaspoon pepper
- 1/8 teaspoon crushed pepper
- 2 teaspoons Italian seasoning
- 1/3 cup fresh basil, chopped

Directions:
1. Switch on the Instant Pot.
2. Select the "Sauté" function. Add oil, onions and garlic and sauté until translucent. Press the "Cancel" button.
3. Add rest of the ingredients except basil.
4. Close the lid. Select the "Steam" function and "Adjust" the timer for down to 3 minutes. Let the steam release naturally.
5. Mix basil and use.

Ragu (Meat Sauce)

Servings: 6
Total time taken: 20-30 min

Ingredients:
- 20 ounces Italian sausage, discard casing
- 2 cloves garlic, peeled
- 1 large red onion, chopped
- 2 cans (14.5 ounces each) chopped tomatoes
- 1 tablespoon dried oregano
- Salt and pepper to taste

Directions:
1. Select the "Sauté" function. Press "Adjust" once for browner. Add sausage and cook until light brown. Break it simultaneously.
2. Add the rest of the ingredients and stir.
3. Press the "Adjust" button once more.
4. Simmer until the liquid dries up.
5. Refrigerate until use.
6. Serve over pasta.

Coffee Barbeque Sauce

Servings: 20-25
Total time taken: 3 hrs. 15 min

Ingredients:
- 2 cups cider vinegar
- 4 cups brewed strong dark coffee
- 2 cups ketchup
- 8 cloves garlic, peeled, crushed
- 2 cups onion, minced
- 2 packed light brown sugar
- 2 jalapeño pepper, deseeded, split
- 6 tablespoons Worcestershire sauce
- 2 cups chicken or beef broth
- 4 tablespoons dry mustard
- 6 tablespoons ground cumin
- 6 tablespoons chili powder or to taste
- Salt to taste

Directions:
1. Add all the ingredients to the inner pot.
2. Switch on the Instant Pot
3. Close the lid. Select the "Slow Cook" option and set the timer for 3 hours.
4. Transfer into an airtight container and refrigerate until use.

Chunky Pork and Mushroom Spaghetti Sauce

Servings: 6
Total time taken: 45 min

Ingredients:
- ¾ pound country style ribs, boneless
- ½ a 29 ounces can tomato puree
- ¼ cup onions, chopped
- ¼ cup bell pepper, chopped
- ¼ cup celery, chopped
- ¼ cup parsley, chopped
- ½ a 14.5 ounces can diced tomatoes with basil, garlic and oregano, with its liquid
- ½ teaspoon fennel seeds
- ½ teaspoon sugar
- 1 ½ cups fresh mushrooms, sliced
- 2 teaspoons olive oil

Directions:
1. Add all the ingredients except oil into the inner pot and stir.
2. Switch on the Instant Pot
3. Close the lid. Select the "Meat" function and use the default time of 35 minutes.
4. When the meat cycle completes, perform a quick release and add oil. Stir and let it cool.
5. Transfer into an airtight container and refrigerate until use.

Sweet Spaghetti Sauce

Servings: 15-18
Total time taken: 2 hrs.

Ingredients:
- 3 cans (29 ounces each) tomato puree
- 1 ½ cans (15 ounces each) tomato paste
- 1 ½ cans (29 ounces each) tomato sauce
- 2 ¼ cups sugar

Directions:
1. Add all the ingredients to the inner pot.
2. Switch on the Instant Pot
3. Close the lid. Select the "Slow Cook" function and set the timer for 2 hours.
4. Store in an airtight container in the refrigerator.
5. It can last for 3-4 days if refrigerated.

Coney Island Hot Dog Sauce

Servings: 12
Total time taken: 3 hrs. 10 min

Ingredients:
- 2 pounds ground beef, browned, broken
- ½ teaspoon garlic, minced
- 1 cup onions, chopped
- 1 cup water
- 30 ounces tomato sauce
- 2 teaspoons Accent seasoning (optional)
- 2 teaspoons chili powder
- 2 teaspoons salt

Directions:
1. Add all the ingredients to the inner pot.
2. Switch on the Instant Pot.
3. Close the lid. Select the "Slow Cook" function and set the timer for 3 hours.
4. Transfer into an airtight container and refrigerate until use.

Italian Tomato Sauce

Servings: 12-15
Total time taken: 2 hrs. 10 min

Ingredients:
- 2 cans (28 ounces each) whole or diced fire roasted tomatoes
- 6 tablespoons olive oil
- 2 cans (6 ounces each) tomato paste
- 2 green bell peppers, diced
- 2 large onions, diced
- 12 cloves garlic, minced
- 2 tablespoons honey
- 2 teaspoons salt or to taste
- Freshly ground black pepper to taste
- 8 teaspoons Italian seasoning

Directions:
1. Switch on the Instant Pot.
2. Select the "Sauté" function. Add oil. When the oil is heated, add onions and bell pepper and sauté until translucent. Press the "Cancel" button.
3. Add the rest of the ingredients and stir.
4. Close the lid. Select the "Slow Cook" function and set the timer for 2 hours.
5. Add parsley. Mix well and remove from heat then let it cool completely.
6. Transfer into an airtight container and refrigerate until use.

Tabasco Sauce

Total time taken: 15 min

Ingredients:
- 1 pound fresh hot peppers of any variety, discard stems, chopped
- 4 teaspoons smoked salt or plain salt
- 2 ½ cups apple cider vinegar

Directions:
1. Add all the ingredients into the inner pot.
2. Switch on the Instant Pot.
3. Close the lid. Select the "Steam" function and use the default time of 10 minutes. Let the pressure release naturally.
4. Blend the ingredients with an immersion blender until smooth.
5. Transfer into a sterilized bottle. Refrigerate until use.

Sriracha Sauce

Total time taken: 1 hr. 15 min

Ingredients:
- ¾ pound fresh red hot jalapeno or Fresno peppers, stemmed, deseeded, chopped
- 2 Thai chilies, stemmed, deseeded, thinly sliced
- 3 cloves garlic
- 1 tablespoon fish sauce
- 1 tablespoon tomato paste
- 1 tablespoon extra virgin olive oil
- 1 ½ tablespoons white wine vinegar
- 1 tablespoon raw honey
- 2 teaspoons salt or to taste

Directions:
1. Add all the ingredients to a blender and blend until smooth. Add a little water if you desire a sauce of thinner consistency.
2. Transfer into the inner pot.
3. Switch on the Instant Pot.
4. Close the lid. Select the "Slow Cook" function and set the timer for 1 hour. Stir in between a couple of times.
5. Let it cool completely then pour into a sterilized jar and store in the refrigerator.

Smoky Mustard Barbeque Sauce

Servings: 10-12
Total time taken: 25 min

Ingredients:
- 2 onions, chopped
- 4 tablespoons vegetable oil
- 2 cloves garlic, minced
- ½ cup tomato ketchup
- 1 cup soft brown sugar
- 2 tablespoons smoked paprika
- Juice of 2 lemons
- 2 teaspoons Dijon mustard
- 2/3 cup Mexican style hot chili sauce
- Freshly cracked black pepper to taste
- Salt or to taste

Directions:
1. Switch on the Instant Pot.
2. Add oil to the inner pot. Select the "Sauté" function.
3. When the oil is heated, add onion and garlic and sauté until translucent.
4. Add the rest of the ingredients except salt and pepper.
5. Press the "Adjust" button twice and simmer for around 10 minutes.
6. Switch off the Instant Pot.
7. Add salt and pepper. Stir and transfer into an airtight container.
8. Refrigerate until use.

Pizza Sauce

Servings: 10-12
Total time taken: 25 min

Ingredients:
- 2 pounds tomatoes, chopped
- ¼ cup garlic, minced
- ¼ cup olive oil + extra to drizzle
- 1 teaspoon dried oregano
- 2 teaspoons salt
- ½ teaspoon red pepper flakes

Directions:
1. Switch on the Instant Pot.
2. Select the "Sauté" function. Add oil. When the oil is heated, add garlic and sauté until golden brown taking care not to brown it.
3. Add the rest of the ingredients and stir. Press the "Cancel" button.
4. Close the lid. Select the "Manual" option and set the timer for 5 minutes. Let the pressure release naturally.
5. Transfer into an airtight container. Drizzle oil and stir.
6. Refrigerate until use.

Bolognese Sauce

Servings: 10-12
Total time taken: 4 hrs. 15 min

Ingredients:
- 1 ½ pounds ground turkey or beef, cubed
- 1 ½ cans (28 ounces each) tomato puree
- 3 small carrots, chopped
- 1 large onion, chopped
- 5 cloves garlic, minced
- 9 ounces canned tomato paste
- 1 ½ tablespoons olive oil
- ¼ teaspoon crushed red pepper flakes or to taste
- 3 teaspoons Italian herb blend
- ¾ teaspoon pepper powder
- ½ teaspoons sea salt
- ¾ cup chicken stock

Directions:
1. Switch on the Instant Pot.
2. Place meat cubes in the inner pot.
3. Mix the rest of the ingredients together in a bowl. Pour over the turkey.
4. Cover and select the "Slow Cook" function and set the timer for the default time of 4 hours.
5. When done, mash with a potato masher and use as required.

CHAPTER 8

Instant Pot Soups & Stews

Creamy Chicken and Mushroom Soup

Servings: 6-8
Total time taken: 45 min

Ingredients:
- 16 ounces portabella mushrooms, sliced
- 10 ounces shiitake mushrooms, sliced
- 14 ounces chicken breast, skinless, chopped
- 2 stalks celery, halved
- 8 cups chicken stock
- 4 teaspoons unsalted butter
- 1 tablespoon fresh parsley, chopped
- ¼ cup flour mixed with ½ cup water

Directions
1. Add all the ingredients to the inner pot.
2. Switch on the Instant Pot
3. Close the lid. Select the "Soup" function and "Adjust" up to 40 minutes. Perform a quick release when the soup cycle is completed.
4. Ladle into soup bowls and serve.

Chicken and Vegetable Soup

Servings: 4
Total time taken: 30 min

Ingredients:
- ¾ pound chicken pieces
- 1 rib celery chopped
- 1 small onion, chopped
- 1 small carrot, chopped
- 1 medium potato, chopped
- 8-10 green beans, stringed, chopped into pieces
- ½ cup pasta
- 4 cups water
- Salt to taste
- 1 tablespoon Italian seasoning

Directions:
1. Switch on the Instant Pot.
2. Add all the ingredients to the inner pot and stir.
3. Close the lid. Select the "Soup" function and "Adjust" down to 20 minutes by pressing the Adjust button twice.
4. Ladle into soup bowls and serve

Spanish Sardines and Tomatoes Soup

Servings: 6
Total time taken: 20 min

Ingredients:
- 9 ounces canned Spanish sardines in tomato sauce and olive oil
- 2 tablespoons olive oil
- 2 large tomatoes, sliced
- 4 cups fresh spinach, chopped
- 2 onions, sliced
- 2 cloves garlic, sliced
- Salt and pepper to taste
- 6 cups water

Directions:
1. Switch on the Instant Pot.
2. Select the "Sauté" function. Add oil, onions, and garlic. Sauté until onions is softened.
3. Add tomatoes and sauté until soft.
4. Add sardines and sauté for a few minutes crushing the sardines simultaneously.
5. Add water, spinach, salt and pepper.
6. Close the lid. Simmer for 5 minutes.

Creamy Crab Soup

Servings: 6
Total time taken: 3 hrs. 15 min

Ingredients:
- 3 cups crab meat, flaked, picked
- 3 cups half and half or evaporated milk
- 3 cups milk
- 4 tablespoons dry sherry
- 5 tablespoons butter
- 4 strips lemon peel
- 4 tablespoons cornstarch mixed with 1/2 cup water
- ¼ teaspoon ground nutmeg
- Salt and pepper to taste
- 1 cup crushed crackers

Directions:
1. Switch on the Instant Pot.
2. Add all the ingredients except sherry, crackers and cornstarch to the inner pot and stir.
3. Close the lid. Select the "Slow cook" function and set the timer for 3 hours.
4. When the Slow cook cycle is over, select the "Sauté" function. Press the Adjust button twice to simmer.
5. Add cornstarch, cracker and sherry and simmer until thick.
6. Ladle into soup bowls and serve.

Hamburger Vegetable Soup

Servings: 8
Total time taken: 40 min

Ingredients:
- 32 ounce ground beef
- 2 cans tomato soup
- 1 cup onions, chopped
- 2 cans (15 ounce each)
- 1 ½ cups frozen corn
- 1 cup frozen peas
- 4 cups potatoes, peeled, cubed
- 1 tablespoon Worcestershire sauce
- 2 cups carrots, sliced
- 3 cups water
- 3 teaspoons dried parsley flakes
- 1 teaspoon olive oil

Directions:
1. Switch on the Instant Pot.
2. Add all the ingredients to the inner pot and stir.
3. Close the lid. Select the "Soup" function and use the default time of 30 minutes.
4. Let the pressure release naturally. Mix well, then let it sit for 5 more minutes.
5. Ladle into bowls and serve.

Beef Potato and Quinoa Soup

Servings: 8-10
Total time taken: 50 min

Ingredients:
- 1 pound beef, cubed
- 2 tablespoons olive oil
- 4 cloves garlic, minced
- 1 small yellow bell pepper, chopped
- 1 large carrot, chopped
- 4 medium potatoes, cubed
- 10 scallions, chopped
- 2 tomatoes, chopped
- 1 teaspoon sazon seasoning
- 2 teaspoons ground cumin
- 10 cups broth
- 2 cups cooked quinoa
- Salt and pepper to taste
- Fresh cilantro to garnish

Directions:
1. Switch on the Instant Pot.
2. Add all the ingredients except the cilantro to the inner pot and stir.
3. Close the lid. Select the "Soup" function and "Adjust" up to 40 minutes.
4. Perform a quick release. Mix well, then let it sit for 5 more minutes.
5. Ladle into bowls, garnish with cilantro and serve.

Pork Cabbage Soup

Servings: 6
Total time taken: 30 min

Ingredients
- 1 ½ pounds lean pork tenderloin, cooked, shredded
- 1 medium head cabbage, shredded
- 1 ½ cans (14.5 ounces each) diced tomatoes
- 2 teaspoons Southwest seasoning
- 3 cups water
- 3 cups chicken stock
- Salt and pepper to taste

Directions:
1. Switch on the Instant Pot.
2. Add all the ingredients to the inner pot.
3. Close the lid. Select the "Soup" function and press the "Adjust" button twice to set the timer down to 20 minutes.
4. When done perform a quick release.
5. Ladle into soup bowls and serve.

Savory Cheese Soup

Servings: 1
Total time taken: 45 min

Ingredients:
- 7 ½ ounces vegetable broth
- 1 tablespoon red bell pepper, chopped
- 1 tablespoon onions, chopped
- 2 tablespoons celery, chopped
- 2 tablespoons carrots, chopped
- 1 teaspoon butter
- Salt to taste
- Pepper powder to serve
- 1 tablespoon all purpose flour mixed with a tablespoon of cold water
- 1 ½ ounces cream cheese, cubed
- 6 tablespoons cheddar cheese, shredded
- 3 tablespoons beer or extra broth
- Croutons to serve

Directions:
1. Switch on the Instant Pot.
2. Add all the ingredients except croutons to the cooking pot and stir.
3. Close the lid. Select the "Soup" function and "Adjust" up to 40 minutes
4. Perform a quick release and open the lid when the soup cycle completes.
5. Ladle into soup bowls and serve with croutons.

Colombian Vegetable Soup

Servings: 4
Total time taken: 25 min

Ingredients:
- 1 medium ear yellow corn, shucked, cut into 6 pieces crosswise
- ¾ pound russet potato, peeled, cubed
- ½ cup frozen peas, divided
- 1 carrot, cubed
- ¾ cup canned fava beans or fresh fava beans, divided
- 3 cups vegetable broth
- Salt and pepper to taste
- Fresh cilantro leaves, chopped

Directions:
1. Switch on the Instant Pot.
2. Add half the fava beans and peas, and rest of the ingredients except cilantro into the Instant Pot.
3. Close the lid. Select the "Manual" option and set the timer for 15 minutes. Perform a quick release when complete.
4. Mash most of the vegetables with a potato masher. Add remaining peas and fava beans and simmer for 5 minutes using the "Sauté" function.
5. Ladle into soup bowls. Place at least 1 corn piece in a bowl.
6. Garnish with cilantro and serve.

Pumpkin and Corn Soup

Servings: 4
Total time taken: 25 min

Ingredients:
- 1 cup frozen corn
- 8 ounces pumpkin puree
- 4 cups broth
- 1 medium onion, chopped
- ½ cup light cream
- Salt and pepper to taste
- ½ teaspoon dried thyme

Directions:
1. Switch on the Instant Pot.
2. Add all the ingredients except cream to inner pot and stir well.
3. Close the lid. Select the "Soup" function and "Adjust" down to 20 minutes.
4. When the cooking cycle is complete, perform a quick release then add cream and stir.
5. Ladle into soup bowls and serve.

Cream of Zucchini Soup

Servings: 6
Total time taken: 35 minutes

Ingredients:
- 5 medium zucchinis, chopped into chunks
- 2 onions, quartered
- 6 cups vegetable stock
- 4 cloves garlic, sliced
- ½ cup coconut milk
- 1 tablespoon ghee or coconut oil
- Freshly ground black pepper
- Salt to taste

Directions:
1. Switch on the Instant Pot.
2. Add all of the ingredients into the inner pot.
3. Close the lid. Select the "Soup" function and use the default time of 30 minutes.
4. Perform a quick release then blend the contents with an immersion blender until smooth.
5. Serve and enjoy.

Vegetable Soup

Servings: 4
Total time taken: 25 min

Ingredients:
- 3 cups vegetable broth
- 1 cup water
- 1 cup cabbage, chopped
- 2 small carrots, peeled, grated
- 1 cup white mushrooms, chopped
- 1 cup zucchini, peeled, chopped
- 1 large onion, chopped
- 1 cup string beans, chopped
- 2 cloves garlic, peeled
- ¼ teaspoon thyme
- ¼ teaspoon Herbes de Province
- Salt to taste
- Pepper powder to taste

Directions:
1. Switch on the Instant Pot.
2. Add all the ingredients to the inner pot.
3. Close the lid. Select the "Soup" function and "Adjust" down to 20 minutes.
4. When the cooking cycle is complete, perform a quick release.
5. Serve and enjoy.

Simple Hamburger Stew

Servings: 6-8
Total time taken: 40 min

Ingredients:
- 2 pounds 90% lean ground beef, browned
- 4 large potatoes, sliced
- 4 medium carrots, sliced
- 4 stalks celery, sliced
- 2 large onions, chopped
- 3 cups frozen peas, thawed
- 2 cans (8 ounces each) tomato sauce
- 2 cans (14.5 ounces each) diced tomatoes with juice
- 4 teaspoons Italian seasoning
- Salt to taste
- Pepper powder to taste

Directions:
1. Switch on the Instant Pot.
2. Add all the ingredients except peas to the instant pot.
3. Close the lid. Select the "Meat/Stew" option and "Adjust" the timer down to 20 minutes.
4. When complete, perform a quick release then add the peas.
5. Serve and enjoy.

Meatball Stew

Servings: 8
Total time taken: 45 min

Ingredients:
- 3 pounds ground beef
- 1 ½ cups green peas, fresh or frozen
- 4 potatoes, peeled, chopped into chunks
- 4 carrots, peeled chopped into chunks
- 4 slices bread, soaked in water for a few seconds and then squeezed
- 2 eggs, lightly beaten
- 4 cloves garlic, minced
- 4 tablespoons fresh parsley, chopped
- 2 teaspoons Worcestershire sauce
- 4 tablespoons olive oil
- 1 teaspoon ground nutmeg
- 1 teaspoon ground black pepper
- 1 teaspoon paprika
- ½ cup white wine
- 2 bay leaves
- A little flour to dust
- 2-3 tablespoons vegetable oil or as required

Directions:
1. Mix together in a large bowl the ground beef and squeezed bread. Add egg, parsley, pepper, garlic, paprika, Worcestershire sauce, 1-tablespoon chicken broth, paprika and nutmeg. Mix well and shape into small meatballs of about 2 inches diameter.
2. Roll the meatballs in flour.
3. Switch on the Instant Pot.
4. Select the "Sauté" option. Add a little oil. When oil is heated, add the meatballs in batches and cook until brown.
5. Add potatoes, carrots, and peas, remaining broth, wine and bay leaves.
6. Close the lid. Select the "Meat/Stew" function and use the default time of 35 minutes. Let the pressure release naturally.
7. Discard the bay leaves.
8. Ladle into bowls and serve hot.

Lemony Garlic Lamb Stew

Servings: 5-6
Total time taken: 40 min

Ingredients:
- 2 pounds lamb stew meat, chopped
- 4 cloves garlic, minced
- 4 teaspoons olive oil
- 1/3 cup chicken stock
- ¼ cup lemon juice
- Salt and pepper to taste

Directions:
1. Switch on the Instant Pot.
2. Select the "Sauté" function. Add oil.
3. When the oil is heated, add lamb to the pot and sauté until brown.
4. Add rest of the ingredients. Mix well.
5. Close the lid. Select the "Meat/Stew" function and use the default time of 35 minutes. Perform a quick release when cooking cycling is complete.
6. Ladle into bowls and serve.

German Style Pork Stew

Servings: 4
Total time taken: 50 minutes

Ingredients:
- 1 pound pork shoulder, boneless, cubed
- ¾ cup apple juice
- ½ pound potatoes, diced
- 1 jar (12 ounces) mushroom gravy
- 1 teaspoon caraway seeds
- Salt to taste
- Pepper to taste

Directions:
1. Switch on the Instant Pot.
2. Add all of the ingredients into the inner pot. Mix well.
3. Close the lid. Select the "Meat/Stew" function and "Adjust" up to 45 minutes. When the cooking cycling is complete, perform a quick release.
4. Ladle into bowls and serve.

Seafood Stew

Servings: 10-12
Total time taken: 25 min

Ingredients:
- 1 pound scallops
- 1 pound large shrimp
- 1 pound crab legs
- 1 ½ pounds baby potatoes
- 1 large onion, chopped
- 1 ½ cans (28 ounce each) crushed tomatoes
- 5 cloves garlic, minced
- 6 cups vegetable broth
- ¾ cup white wine
- 1 ½ teaspoons dried basil
- 1 ½ teaspoons dried thyme
- 1 ½ teaspoons dried cilantro
- ¾ teaspoon celery salt
- ½ teaspoon red pepper flakes
- 1/4 teaspoon cayenne pepper

Directions:
1. Switch on the Instant Pot.
2. Add all of the ingredients into the inner pot. Mix well.
3. Close the lid. Select the "Meat/Stew" function and "Adjust" down to 20 minutes. When the cooking cycling is complete, perform a quick release.
4. Ladle into bowls and serve.

Vegetarian Stew

Servings: 12
Total time taken: 25 minutes

Ingredients:
- 4 mushrooms, chopped
- 2 cups frozen peas
- 2 leeks, sliced
- 5 large carrots, peeled, sliced
- 4 celery ribs, sliced
- 6 russet potatoes, peeled, cubed
- 2 packages (8 ounces each) seitan, sliced, browned
- 2 teaspoons Worcestershire sauce
- 2 teaspoons canola oil
- 8 cups water
- 2 teaspoons Herbes de Provence
- ¼ cup flour mixed in ¼ cup water
- Salt and pepper to taste

Directions:
1. Switch on the Instant Pot.
2. Add all of the ingredients into the inner pot. Mix well.
3. Close the lid. Select the "Meat/Stew" function and "Adjust" down to 20 minutes. When the cooking cycling is complete, perform a quick release.
4. Ladle into bowls and serve.

Easy Chili

Servings: 2
Total time taken: 40 min

Ingredients:
- ½ pound ground beef or turkey
- 1 can (15 ounces) beans of your choice, drained
- 1 small onion, chopped
- 1 ½ cans (15 ounces each) diced tomatoes with green chilies
- 1 tablespoon chili powder
- Sour cream and green onions to garnish

Directions:
1. Switch on the Instant Pot.
2. Add all of the ingredients into the inner pot. Mix well.
3. Close the lid. Select the "Meat/Stew" function and use the default time of 35 minutes. When the cooking cycling is complete, perform a quick release.
4. Ladle into bowls and serve.

Vegetarian Chili

Servings: 2-3
Total time taken: 35 min

Ingredients:
- ½ 19 ounce can low sodium black bean soup
- ½ 15 ounce can of each kidney beans, garbanzo beans, drained and vegetarian baked beans
- 7 ounces pureed tomatoes
- ½ 15 ounce can whole corn kernels, drained
- 1 onion, chopped
- ½ green bell pepper, chopped
- ½ red bell pepper, chopped
- 1 stalk celery, chopped
- 2 cloves garlic, chopped
- Salt and chili powder to taste
- ½ tablespoon dried oregano
- ½ tablespoon dried parsley
- ½ tablespoon dried basil

Directions:
1. Switch on the Instant Pot.
2. Add all of the ingredients into the inner pot. Mix well.
3. Close the lid. Select the "Chili" function and use the default time of 30 minutes. When the cooking cycling is complete, perform a quick release.
4. Ladle into bowls and serve.

CHAPTER 9

Instant Pot Snack Recipes

BBQ Chicken Drummies

Servings: 3
Total time taken: 2 hrs. 10 min

Ingredients:
- 1 ½ pounds chicken drummies, thawed, pat dried
- 2 tablespoons honey
- 1 tablespoon chili sauce
- ¾ cup barbecue sauce
- 2 cloves garlic, minced
- Salt and pepper to taste

Directions:
1. Switch on the Instant Pot.
2. Add all the ingredients to the inner pot and stir.
3. Close the lid. Select the "Slow Cook" function and timer for 2 hours.
4. Serve and enjoy.

Honey Garlic Chicken Wings

Servings: 10
Total time taken: 3 hrs.

Ingredients:
- 20 chicken wings
- 10 tablespoons raw honey
- 1 tablespoon olive oil
- Salt and pepper to taste

Directions:
1. Switch on the Instant Pot.
2. Place the chicken wings in the inner pot.
3. Mix together in a small bowl the rest of the ingredients. Pour over the chicken wings. Mix well as to coat all the pieces.
4. Close the lid. Select the "Slow Cook" function and set the timer for 3 hours.

Chicken Paprika

Servings: 6
Total time taken: 20 min

Ingredients:
6 chicken breasts, skinless, boneless, chop into chunks
- 4 tablespoons olive oil
- 4 tablespoons Spanish smoked paprika
- 3 tablespoons lemon juice
- 1 ½ tablespoons maple syrup
- 3 teaspoons garlic, minced
- Salt to taste
- Pepper powder to taste

Directions:
1. Switch on the Instant Pot.
2. Mix together all the ingredients in a bowl except the chicken to make the sauce.
3. Season the chicken with salt and pepper. Pour 1/3 of the sauce in the bottom of the Instant Pot and place chicken in it.
4. Pour the remaining sauce all over the chicken pieces.
5. Close the lid. Select the "Poultry" function and use the default time of 15 minutes.

Sweet n Spicy Meatballs

Servings: 20-25
Total time taken: 15-20 min

Ingredients:
- 3 pounds cooked, frozen meatballs, thawed
- 3 cups chili sauce or cocktail sauce
- 1 ½ cups grape or apple jelly

Directions:
1. Switch on the Instant Pot.
2. Mix together jelly and chili sauce in a bowl.
3. Place the meatballs in the inner pot. Pour the jelly mixture over it.
4. Close the lid. Select the "Sauté" function. Press the Adjust button twice to simmer.
5. Simmer until the sauce is thick and well coated around the meatballs, this should take approximately 15 minutes. Insert toothpicks and serve.

BBQ Ribs

Servings: 4
Total time taken: 45 min

Ingredients:
- 2 racks baby back ribs, remove membrane from back of the rib with paper towel
- Salt and pepper to taste
- ½ cup BBQ sauce

Directions:
1. Switch on the Instant Pot.
2. Sprinkle salt and pepper over the ribs.
3. Pour a cup of water into the inner pot and place a trivet. Place ribs over the trivet.
4. Close the lid. Select the "Meat" function and "Adjust" down to 20 minutes.
5. Remove contents from the pot and place in a baking dish. Pour BBQ over the ribs and toss.
6. Bake in a preheated oven at 450 degree F for 10-15 minutes and serve.

BBQ Smoked Sausage

Servings: 5-6
Total time taken: 15 minutes

Ingredients:
- 1 ½ pounds smoked sausages, chopped into 1 inch pieces
- ¾ tablespoon brown sugar
- Sweet BBQ sauce as required
- 1 tablespoon lemon juice

Directions:
1. Switch on the Instant Pot.
2. Place sausages in the inner pot. Submerge with water.
3. Close the lid. Select the "Manual" option and set the timer for 10 minutes. Quick release excess pressure. Drain and transfer into bowl.
4. Mix together rest of the ingredients in a bowl and pour over sausages. Insert toothpicks and serve.

Chinese Boiled Peanuts

Servings: 6-8
Total time taken: 30 min

Ingredients:
- 2 pounds large raw green peanuts
- 2 chunks rock sugar
- 4 star anise
- 6 cloves garlic
- 4 sticks cinnamon
- 8 dried red chili peppers (optional)

Directions:
1. Switch on the Instant Pot.
2. Add all the ingredients to inner pot. Submerge with water.
3. Close the lid. Select the "Manual" option and set the timer for 25 minutes.
4. Quick release, cool, and serve.

Meatballs

Servings: 6
Total time taken: 45 min

Ingredients:
- ¾ pound ground beef
- 1 small onion, minced
- ¼ cup uncooked rice
- ½ cup tomato juice
- 1/3 cup water

Directions:
1. Switch on the Instant Pot.
2. Add water and tomato juice to the inner pot.
3. Mix together rest of the ingredients and shape into small balls. Lower the balls into the pot.
4. Close the lid. Select the "Meat/Stew" function and use the default time of 35 minutes.
5. Perform a quick release. Insert toothpicks and serve.

Steamed Corn

Servings: 4
Total time taken: 20 min

Ingredients:
- 2 cups frozen corn
- 2 tablespoons butter
- ½ teaspoon oregano
- Salt to taste
- Pepper to taste
- ¼ teaspoon red chili flakes
- 2 tablespoons lemon juice
- 1 small green bell pepper, finely chopped
- 1 red bell pepper, finely chopped

Directions:
1. Switch on the Instant Pot.
2. Pour 1 cup water in the inner pot. Place a steamer basket in and put corn in the basket.
3. Close the lid. Select the "Steam" function and "Adjust" up to 15 minutes.
4. Perform a quick release and transfer into a bowl. Add rest of the ingredients and serve.

Loaded Potato Skins

Servings: 8
Total time taken: 3-4 hrs.

Ingredients:
- 8 medium potatoes, rinsed
- 2 tablespoons chives, chopped
- 4 tablespoons butter
- 4 tablespoons sour cream
- Salt to taste
- Pepper powder to taste
- Cooking spray

Directions:
1. Spray the inside of the inner pot with cooking spray.
2. Prick each of the potatoes with a fork (all over) and place in the pot.
3. Switch on the Instant Pot.
4. Close the lid. Select the "Slow Cook" function and set the timer for 3-4 hours.
5. Remove from the pot and cool. When cool enough to handle, halve the potatoes with a fork.
6. Lightly fluff the inside part of the potatoes with the fork.
7. Top the potatoes with the rest of the ingredients and serve warm.

Dhokla

Servings: 12-15
Total time taken: 35 min

Ingredients:
- 3 cups chickpea flour (garbanzo) flour
- ¼ teaspoon asafetida
- 4 teaspoons fruit salt
- 1 teaspoon sugar
- 1 teaspoon salt
- 1 teaspoon turmeric powder
- ½ teaspoon chili powder
- 2 green chilies, finely chopped
- 2 cups water
- 2 tablespoons cilantro, chopped to garnish
- ¼ cup fresh grated coconut (optional) to garnish

For tempering:
- 2 teaspoons mustard seeds
- 2 teaspoons oil
- 10-12 curry leaves
- 1 cup water
- 2 tablespoons lemon juice

Directions:
1. Mix together in a bowl the garbanzo flour, asafetida, salt, sugar, chili powder, green chilies and water. Whisk until well combined and ensure there are no lumps. Set aside.
2. Switch on the Instant Pot.
3. Grease a heatproof container that fits into the inner pot. Pour 1 ½ cups water into the pot and place a trivet. Place the container on the trivet.
4. Mix fruit salt into the batter and stir vigorously for a minute and pour the batter into the container that is placed in the pot.
5. Select the "Steam" function.
6. Close the lid and "Adjust" up to 15 minutes.
7. Meanwhile, place a small deep pan over medium heat. Add oil. When oil heats, add mustard seeds. When it crackles, add curry leaves and sauté for a couple of minutes. Add water and lemon juice and bring to the boil. Simmer for a few minutes.
8. Remove the container from the pot. Pour this mixture over the container contents. Chop into squares.
9. Cover and set-aside until cold. Garnish cilantro and fresh coconut and serve.

Caponatina

Servings: 3
Total time taken: 20 min

Ingredients:
- 1 large potato, cubed
- 1 onion, chopped into wedges
- 1 large eggplant, cubed
- 1 medium bell pepper, cubed
- 1 medium zucchini, sliced into thick rounds
- 6 cherry tomatoes, halved
- A handful pine nuts
- ¼ cup olive oil
- ½ tablespoons capers
- ½ tablespoon raisins, soaked in water
- 1 cup basil, chopped
- 2 tablespoons green olives, pitted
- Salt and pepper to taste

Directions:
1. Sprinkle salt over the eggplant.
2. Switch on the Instant Pot.
3. Select the "Sauté" function and add oil to the inner pot. Add the eggplant and sauté for 3 minutes. Add the rest of the ingredients and sauté for 2 minutes. Then add ½ cup water, salt, and pepper.
4. Close the lid. Select the "Steam" function and use the default time of 10 minutes. Quick release the steam.
5. Stir and serve.

Pressure Cooked Red Potatoes

Servings: 8
Total time taken: 5 min

Ingredients:
- 1 ½ pounds small red potatoes, washed, peeled, cubed
- 1 cup water
- ½ teaspoon olive oil
- 2 tablespoons butter
- Salt to taste
- Pepper powder to taste

Directions:
1. Switch on the Instant Pot.
2. Pour oil and water in the pot. Place a steamer basket in and place potatoes on it.
3. Close the lid. Select the "Steam" function and use the default time of 10 minutes.
4. When done, quick release the pressure.
5. Remove the potatoes from the pot and transfer into a bowl. Add butter, salt and pepper. Mix well and serve.

Hummus

Servings: 10-12
Total time taken: 7 hrs. 30 min

Ingredients:
- 2 ½ cups dried chickpeas, soaked in water for at least 6-7 hours
- 4 teaspoons olive oil
- Salt to taste
- Water as required
- 1 cup tahini
- 4 cloves garlic
- ½ teaspoon ground cumin + extra to garnish
- ½ cup lemon juice
- ½ cups olive oil
- 1 teaspoon salt

Directions:
1. Switch on the Instant Pot.
2. Add chickpeas and a teaspoon salt to the inner pot. Add enough water such that the water is about 2-3 inches above the chickpeas.
3. Close the lid. Select the "Steam" function and "Adjust" the timer up to 15 minutes.
4. Strain and retain some of the cooked liquid.
5. Blend together retained liquid and rest of the ingredients except ¼ cup oil until smooth.
6. Transfer into a bowl. Drizzle the remaining olive oil. Sprinkle a little cumin powder on top.
7. Serve with vegetable sticks or falafels or pita bread.

Spicy Sweet Potatoes

Servings: 6
Total time taken: 20 min

Ingredients:
- 6 medium sweet potatoes, rinsed
- ½ teaspoon red chili flakes
- Salt to taste
- 2 tablespoons lemon juice

Directions:
1. Pour about a cup of water into the inner pot. Place a steamer basket in it.
2. Switch on the Instant Pot.
3. Prick the sweet potatoes with a fork all over. Place the sweet potatoes over the steamer basket.
4. Close the lid. Select the "Steam" function and "Adjust" the timer to up 15 minutes.
5. When the timer goes off, let the steam release naturally for 10 minutes.
6. Peel the sweet potatoes. Sprinkle chili flakes, salt and lemon juice over it and serve.

Asian Sesame Carrots

Servings: 4
Total time taken: 20 min

Ingredients:
- 2 large carrots, chopped into chunks
- 2 teaspoons grated ginger
- 4 teaspoons toasted sesame seeds
- 2 chopped scallions
- 2 tablespoons sesame oil
- 3 teaspoons soy sauce
- 3 teaspoons rice vinegar
- Salt and pepper to taste

Directions:
1. Switch on the Instant Pot.
2. Add all the ingredients except sesame to the cooking pot.
3. Close the lid. Select the "Steam" function and use the default time of 10 minutes.
4. If there is liquid in it, simmer until dry using "Sauté." Add sesame seeds and stir.
5. Insert toothpicks and serve.

Garlic Potatoes

Servings: 8-10
Total time taken: 1 hr. 20 min

Ingredients:
- 1 ½ tablespoons garlic paste
- 1 ½ pounds baby potatoes, scrubbed, pricked with fork
- 1 ½ tablespoons tamarind paste
- ¾ teaspoon red chili paste
- 1 teaspoon salt
- 2 teaspoons oil

Directions:
1. Switch on the Instant Pot.
2. Select the "Sauté" function. Add oil and all the ingredients except potatoes and sauté until fragrant. Press the Cancel button.
3. Add potatoes and ¼ cup water.
4. Close the lid. Select the "Slow Cook" function and set the timer for 1 hour. Uncover and simmer until dry. Insert toothpicks and serve

Spicy Chickpeas

Servings: 4
Total time taken: 35 min

Ingredients:
- 2 cups garbanzo beans, soaked in water overnight
- 1 teaspoon cumin seeds
- 1 teaspoon salt
- 1 teaspoon chili powder
- 2 teaspoons oil
- 1 onion, minced
- 2 tablespoons fresh cilantro
- 2 tablespoons lemon juice

Directions:
1. Switch on the Instant Pot.
2. Select the "Sauté" function. Add oil and cumin. When the cumin crackles add chickpeas, salt, and chili powder. Add water to cover an inch above the beans. Close the lid. Select the "Bean/Chili" function and "Adjust" down to 25 minutes.
3. Let the pressure release naturally. Add rest of the ingredients and stir well. Spoon into bowls and serve.

Cheesy Mushrooms

Servings: 6
Total time taken: 15 minutes

Ingredients:
- 4 cups medium sized button mushrooms
- 1 cup cheese, grated
- Salt to taste
- Pepper powder to taste
- 4 tablespoons lemon juice
- 1 tablespoon olive oil
- Hot water

Directions:
1. Switch on the Instant Pot.
2. Select the "Sauté" option. Add oil. When the oil is heated, add mushrooms and sauté for about 5 minutes.
3. Add 2 tablespoons of lemon juice, salt, pepper and cheese and sauté for another 5 minutes.
4. Transfer onto a serving platter. Sprinkle lemon juice over it. Insert toothpicks and serve.

Root Medley

Servings: 2
Total time taken: 30 min

Ingredients:
- 2 beetroots, peeled, cubed
- 2 carrots, cubed
- 2 turnips, cubed
- 1 large onion, chopped
- 2 teaspoons oil
- 1 green chili, slit
- 1 teaspoon whole cumin
- 2 tomatoes, chopped
- 1 teaspoon salt

Directions:
1. Switch on the Instant Pot.
2. Select the "Sauté" function. Add oil and cumin. When the cumin crackles, add onions and sauté until translucent. Add rest of the ingredients and ½ cup water. Press the Cancel button.
3. Close the lid. Select the "Steam" function and use the default time of 10 minutes.
4. Perform a quick release. Simmer until nearly dry, then serve and enjoy.

CHAPTER 10

Instant Pot Meat Recipes

Spicy Drumsticks

Servings: 8
Total time taken: 3 hrs. 45 min

Ingredients:
- 8 chicken drumsticks
- 1 cup picante sauce
- 4 teaspoon cayenne pepper sauce or ¼ teaspoon cayenne pepper powder
- 1 teaspoon smoked paprika
- ½ teaspoon dried thyme, crushed
- 2 bay leaves
- 1 ½ tablespoons olive oil
- Cooking spray

Directions:
1. Switch on the Instant Pot.
2. Spray the inside of the cooking pot with cooking spray.
3. In a small bowl, mix together picante sauce, cayenne pepper sauce, thyme and bay leaf.
4. Place the chicken in the pot. Spread the sauce mixture over the chicken. Cover and keep aside for about 30 minutes to marinate.
5. Select the "Slow Cook" function and set the timer for 3 hours. Close the lid.
6. Discard the bay left. Remove the chicken and place in a serving bowl. Add oil to the remaining sauce in the cooker and mix well. Spread this sauce over the chicken. Cover and keep aside for 15 minutes and serve.

Slow Cooked Chicken

Servings: 2-4
Total time taken: 3 hrs. 15 min

Ingredients:
- 1 small whole chicken, cleaned, pat dried
- 2 carrots, peeled, cut into pieces
- 1 stalk celery, chopped
- 1 medium onion, chopped
- 4 cloves garlic, peeled
- 1 tablespoon Herbes de Provence
- Salt to taste
- Black pepper powder to taste
- Juice of a lemon

Directions:
1. Switch on the Instant Pot.
2. Stuff the chicken with garlic.
3. Sprinkle the chicken all over with salt, pepper and Herbes de Provence.
4. Place the vegetables at the bottom of the instant pot.
5. Place the chicken over the vegetables.
6. Close the lid. Select the "Slow Cook" function and set the timer for 3 hours.
7. Sprinkle lemon juice and serve hot.

Creamy Chicken and Mushroom Potpie

Servings: 8
Total time taken: 3 hrs. 45 min

Ingredients:
- 16 ounces cremini mushrooms, stems trimmed, halved if the mushrooms are large
- 8 carrots, peeled, cut into 1 inch pieces
- 3 pounds chicken thighs, skinless, boneless
- 1 large onion, chopped
- 2/3 cup all-purpose flour
- 2 sheets puff pastry, thawed
- 2 cups frozen green beans
- 2 cups frozen green peas
- 2 bay leaves
- 1 teaspoon dried thyme
- 1 cup water
- Salt to taste
- Pepper powder to taste
- ¼ cup cream

Directions:
1. Switch on the Instant Pot.
2. Add onions, mushrooms, carrots, onion, all-purpose flour, thyme, bay leaves and water to the cooking pot. Stir well.
3. Lay the chicken thighs over the vegetable mixture. Sprinkle salt and pepper over the chicken as well as over the vegetables.
4. Close the lid. Select the "Slow Cook" function and set the timer for 3 ½ hours.
5. When done, switch off the Instant Pot and keep it covered.
6. Cut pastry sheets with a 4-½ inch cutter into 4 circles. Place the circles on a baking sheet and bake in a preheated oven at 425 degree F for about 8 – 10 minutes.
7. Just before serving, add peas, green beans, cream and salt to the Instant Pot. Cover and heat the contents thoroughly.
8. Divide and serve chicken along with vegetables in individual serving bowls. Place a baked pastry round over each bowl and serve.

Chicken Risotto

Servings: 6
Total time taken: 45 min

Ingredients:
- 3 cups Arborio rice, rinsed
- 6 cups vegetable broth
- 1 large onion, thinly sliced
- 4 cloves garlic, minced
- 1 ½ pounds mushrooms, sliced
- 3 cups baby spinach
- 3 chicken thighs, sliced
- ¼ cup butter
- ¼ cup olive oil
- ¾ cup dry white wine
- 3 tablespoons Krush spice mix or Italian spice blend
- 2 teaspoons salt

Directions:
1. Switch on the Instant Pot.
2. Select the "Sauté" function. Add oil and half the butter to the pot. Add onions and garlic. Sauté until the onions are translucent. Press the Adjust button once.
3. Add chicken and continue to sauté until brown. Add krush mix and sauté until fragrant.
4. Add mushroom and rice to the pot. Mix well until the rice is well coated with the oil. Add white wine and vegetable broth.
5. Close the lid. Select the "Rice" function.
6. Perform a quick release. Add remaining butter and cheese. Mix well and serve.

Seasoned Chicken, Potatoes & Green Beans

Servings: 8
Total time taken: 4 hrs. 25 min

Ingredients:
- 3 pounds chicken breasts, skinless, boneless
- 1 ¾ pounds red potatoes, cubed
- ¾ pound green beans, trimmed
- 4 cloves garlic, minced
- 1/3 cup olive oil
- ½ cup fresh lemon juice
- Salt and pepper to taste
- ½ teaspoon onion powder
- 1 ½ teaspoons dried oregano

Directions:
1. Switch on the Instant Pot.
2. Place the chicken in the center of the cooking pot. Place the beans all around the chicken then the potatoes over the chicken.
3. Whisk together rest of the ingredients in a bowl and pour over the chicken.
4. Close the lid. Select the "Slow Cook" function use the default timer of 4 hours.

Chicken Paprikash

Servings: 2
Total time taken: 25 min

Ingredients:
- 1 pound chicken breast, skinless, boneless, cut into ½ inch strips
- 1 cup onion, chopped
- 2 teaspoons garlic, minced (preferably minced)
- 1 medium carrot, shredded
- 4 ounce mushrooms, sliced
- 1 medium red bell pepper, chopped
- 1 tablespoon Hungarian sweet paprika
- 1 ½ tablespoons all-purpose flour
- ¾ cup low sodium chicken broth
- Salt to taste
- Pepper powder to taste
- ¾ cup sour cream

Directions:
1. Switch on the Instant Pot.
2. Place the chicken in a bowl and sprinkle flour all over it and coat it well. Transfer to the inner pot.
3. Add the rest of the ingredients except sour cream. Stir.
4. Close the lid. Select the "Poultry" function and use the default time of 15 minutes.
5. Perform a quick release. Add sour cream, stir and serve.

Turkey Osso Buco

Servings: 3
Total time taken: 45 minutes

Ingredients:
- 1 whole turkey leg, cut at joints into drumsticks and thighs, skinless
- ½ teaspoon dried thyme
- 1 medium onion, chopped
- 1 medium carrot, peeled, chopped
- 4 cloves garlic, minced, divided
- 1 stalk celery, chopped
- ½ tablespoon olive oil
- ¼ cup dry red wine
- 14 ounce canned, diced tomatoes along with juice
- 2 tablespoons fresh Italian parsley, chopped
- ½ teaspoon lemon zest, grated
- Salt to taste
- Pepper powder to taste

Directions:
1. Switch on the Instant Pot.
2. Crush dried thyme and rub it all over the turkey. Season with salt and pepper. Set aside.
3. Select the "Sauté" function. Add oil. When the oil is heated, add onions, carrots, celery, and sauté for a few minutes until onions are translucent. Add half the garlic, sauté for a few minutes until fragrant. Add wine and boil for a few seconds. Scrape any browned bits that may be stuck to the bottom of the pot. Press the "Cancel" button. Transfer into a bowl and set aside.
4. Place turkey in the cooking pot. Pour the vegetable mixture over it. Add tomatoes along with the juices.
5. Close the lid. Select the "Poultry" function and "Adjust" the timer up to 30 minutes.
6. Mix together in a small bowl, parsley, lemon zest, and remaining garlic. Add salt and pepper, mix well and keep aside.
7. Perform a quick release then remove the turkey from the pot with a slotted spoon. When cool enough to handle, pull apart the meat from the bones with a pair of forks and serve in individual bowls. Top with vegetables and its liquid from the pot. Sprinkle the parsley mixture over it and serve.

Mediterranean Roast Turkey

Servings: 3-4
Total time taken: 3 hrs. 40 min

Ingredients:
- 1 cup onions, chopped
- ¼ cup julienne cut, oil packed sun dried tomato halves drained
- ¼ cup Kalamata olives, pitted
- 1 teaspoon garlic, minced
- 1 tablespoon fresh lemon juice
- ½ teaspoon Greek seasoning mix
- ¼ teaspoon salt
- Freshly ground black pepper powder to taste
- 2 pound turkey breast, boneless, trimmed
- ¼ cup fat free, low sodium chicken broth, divided
- 1 ½ tablespoons all-purpose flour
- A few sprigs of thyme

Directions:
1. Switch on the Instant Pot.
2. Add all the ingredients except flour and half the chicken broth to the cooking pot.
3. Close the lid. Select the "Slow Cook" function and set the timer for 3 ½ hours.
4. Meanwhile, mix together flour and the remaining broth until smooth. Pour into the cooker. Stir well, cover and select the "Poultry" function and "Adjust" the timer up to 30 minutes.
5. When done, perform a quick release then chop the turkey into slices and serve.

Korean Beef

Servings: 3
Total time taken: 1 hr.

Ingredients:
- 1 ½ pounds beef chuck roast, cut into 1 inch cubes
- ½ cup beef broth
- ¼ cup low sodium sauce
- ¼ cup brown sugar, packed
- ½ tablespoon sesame oil
- 2 cloves garlic, minced
- ¼ tablespoon fresh ginger, grated
- ½ tablespoon rice wine vinegar
- 1 teaspoon Sriracha sauce or to taste
- ½ teaspoon onion powder
- ¼ teaspoon white pepper powder
- 1 tablespoon cornstarch
- 2 tablespoons water
- ½ teaspoon sesame seeds
- 1 green onion, thinly sliced

Directions:
1. Switch on the Instant Pot.
2. Place the chuck roast in the cooking pot. Mix together in a bowl, beef broth, soy sauce, brown sugar, garlic, sesame oil, vinegar, ginger, onion powder, Sriracha sauce and white powder. Pour this mixture into the pot and stir.
3. Close the lid. Select the "Meat/Stew" function and "Adjust" the timer up to 45 minutes. Then perform a quick release.
4. Next, whisk together cornstarch and water. Add to the pot. Mix well and close the lid. Select Sauté option and press the Adjust button twice. Cook until the sauce thickens.
5. Serve garnished with sesame seeds and green onions.

Thai Red Curry

Servings: 3
Total time taken: 55 min

Ingredients:
- 1 ½ pounds lean beef stew meat
- Salt to taste
- 1 ½ cups onions, finely chopped
- 3 cloves garlic, minced
- ½ cup low sodium beef broth
- ½ tablespoon dark brown sugar
- 2 tablespoons red curry paste
- 1 ½ tablespoons fish sauce
- 1 ½ tablespoons fresh lime juice
- 10 ounce canned light coconut milk
- 2 cups baby spinach
- ¼ cup fresh basil leaves

Directions:
1. Switch on the Instant Pot.
2. Select the "Sauté" function and press the "Adjust" button once. Add beef and cook until brown. Set aside and season with salt.
3. Add onions and garlic to the pot and sauté for a few minutes until the onions are translucent. Press Cancel button.
4. Place beef in the pot. Spread this mixture over the beef.
5. Mix together rest of the ingredients in a bowl and pour it over and around the beef.
6. Close the lid. Select the "Meat/Stew" function and use the default time of 35 minutes.
7. Select the "Sauté" function. Press the Adjust button twice. Add spinach and simmer for 15 minutes.
8. Sprinkle basil leaves.
9. Serve with brown rice.

Beef Nachos

Servings: 4
Total time taken: 4 hrs. 10 min

Ingredients:
- 1 ½ pounds beef rump roast
- ½ 12 ounce jar mild banana pepper rings
- ½ 15 ounce can beef broth
- ½ tablespoon olive oil
- 2 cloves garlic, minced
- ½ 15 ounce can black beans, rinsed
- 1 large ripe tomato, chopped
- 1 large onion, finely chopped
- Monterey Jack cheese, shredded to serve
- Tortilla chips to serve
- Sour cream to serve
- 2 tablespoons fresh cilantro, chopped
- 1 avocado, peeled, pitted, thinly sliced
- Salt to taste
- Pepper powder to taste

Directions:
1. Switch on the Instant Pot.
2. Sprinkle roast with salt and pepper.
3. Select the "Sauté" function. Press the Adjust button once. Add roast and cook until brown.
4. Add banana pepper rings, broth and garlic.
5. Close the lid. Select the "Slow Cook" function and set the timer for 4 hours.
6. Perform a quick release then remove roast and place on your cutting board. When cool enough to handle, shred the meat and transfer it back to the pot. Stir and cook for another 5-7 minutes using "Sauté."
7. Meanwhile, lay tortilla chips on a baking sheet. Layer the chips with shredded beef, black beans, followed by tomatoes and onions and finally cheese.
8. Bake in a preheated oven at 350 degree F for about 10 minutes.
9. Garnish with cilantro and sour cream. Serve with avocado.

American Meat Loaf

Servings: 4 - 5
Total time taken: 3 hrs. 15 min

Ingredients:
- 3 pounds ground chuck roast
- 1 small onion, chopped
- 1 small green bell pepper, chopped
- 2 eggs, beaten
- ½ cup milk
- 3 teaspoons salt or to taste
- 4 slices bread, made into crumbs
- 12 medium potatoes, cubed
- ¼ cup celery, chopped
- 2-3 tablespoons ketchup

Directions:
1. Switch on the Instant Pot.
2. Mix together all the ingredients except potatoes and ketchup. Using your hands, shape the dough into a loaf and place it in the instant pot.
3. Brush with ketchup.
4. Lay the potato pieces around the sides of the loaf.
5. Close the lid. Select the "Slow Cook" function and set for 3 hours.
6. Slice and serve warm.

Italian Beef

Servings: 3
Total time taken: 40 minutes

Ingredients:
- 1 ½ pounds beef chuck roast
- 1 ½ dry Italian salad dressing mix
- ½ cup water
- 8 ounce jar pepperoncini peppers
- 4 hamburger buns, split

Directions:
1. Switch on the Instant Pot.
2. Place the beef chuck roast in the cooking pot.
3. Add the Italian dressing mix.
4. Pour water.
5. Close the lid. Select the "Meat/Stew" function and use the default time of 35 minutes option.
6. Perform a quick release then remove the roast form the pot. When cool enough to handle, the shred the meat.
7. Add the peppers and some of the juice (optional).
8. Serve over the split buns.

Easter Sunday Pot Roast

Servings: 4
Total time taken: 50 minutes

Ingredients:

For sauce:
- ½ packet instant gravy powder
- ½ packet instant ranch dip powder
- 1 cup beef broth
- 1 shallot, sliced
- 1 tablespoon Worcestershire sauce

For roast:
- 2 pounds beef rump roast
- 1 cup red potatoes, chopped
- 1 cup carrots, chopped
- 1 cup mushrooms, sliced
- ½ cup onions, sliced

Directions:
1. Switch on the Instant Pot.
2. Add all the ingredients of the sauce to cooking pot. Mix well.
3. Place the chuck roast and the vegetables in it. Mix well.
4. Close the lid. Select the "Meat/Stew" function and "Adjust" the timer up to 45 minutes.
5. Perform a quick release then serve and enjoy.

Ragu with Ground Sirloin

Servings: 4
Total time taken: 25 minutes

Ingredients:
- 1 ½ pounds lean ground sirloin
- 3 ounces penne pasta
- 1 ½ jars 4 cheese sauce
- 1 ½ jars water
- 2 cloves garlic, minced
- Salt to taste
- Pepper to taste

Directions:
1. Select the "Sauté" function. Press the Adjust button once.
2. Add sirloin to the cooking pot. Cook until brown.
3. Add rest of the ingredients.
4. Close lid. Select the "Meat/Stew" function and "Adjust" down to 20 minutes.
5. When done, quick release excess pressure. Serve and enjoy.

Spaghetti Squash and Meatballs

Servings: 4
Total time taken: 3 hrs. 10 min

Ingredients:
- 2 pounds ground Italian sausage
- 2 medium spaghetti squash, halved, deseeded
- 2 cans (14 ounce each) tomato sauce
- 1 teaspoon dried oregano
- 1 teaspoon thyme
- 8 cloves garlic, whole
- 1 teaspoon dried basil
- 4 tablespoon hot pepper relish (optional)
- 4 tablespoons olive oil
- 2 tablespoons fresh parsley, chopped

Directions:
1. Switch on the Instant Pot.
2. Add olive oil, tomato sauce, garlic, hot pepper relish, oregano, basil, and thyme to the cooking pot. Mix well.
3. Place the spaghetti squash halves in the pot with its cut side down.
4. Meanwhile, make small meatballs with the ground meat and place it all around the squash.
5. Close the lid. Select the "Slow Cook" function and set the timer for 3 hours.
6. When done, remove the squash from the pot. When cool enough to handle, pull out the flesh from the squash using a large fork.
7. Place the squash flesh on a serving platter. Top with the meatballs. Pour the sauce all over. Garnish with parsley and serve hot.

Portuguese Chorizo and Peppers

Servings: 6
Total time taken: 50 min

Ingredients:
- 3 pounds chorizo sausage, discard casings, crumbled
- 3 sweet onion, peeled, chopped
- 3 tablespoons garlic, crushed
- 3 green bell peppers, deseeded, chopped
- 1 ½ cans (6 ounces each) tomato paste
- 1 ½ cups water
- 1 ½ cups red wine

Directions:
1. Switch on the Instant Pot.
2. Add all the ingredients into the cooking pot.
3. Close the lid. Select the "Meat/Stew" function and "Adjust" the timer up to 45 minutes.
4. Serve over rice or rolls.

Super Easy Country Style Ribs

Servings: 2
Total time taken: 4 hrs. 20 minutes

Ingredients:
- 1 pound country style pork ribs, boneless
- ¾ cup ketchup
- ¼ cup vinegar
- ¼ cup brown sugar
- ¼ teaspoon liquid smoke
- 1 teaspoon seasoned salt

Directions:
1. Switch on the Instant Pot.
2. Add all the ingredients into the cooking pot.
3. Close the lid. Select the "Slow Cook" function and use the default time of 4 hours.
4. Remove the ribs with a slotted spoon and place on a serving platter. Set aside for 10 minutes. Discard the fat that will float on top.
5. Select the "Sauté" function and simmer until the gravy is thickened.
6. Slice the roast. Pour sauce over the roast and serve.

Mexican Posole

Servings: 6
Total time taken: 45 min

Ingredients:
- 1 pound pork loin roast, boneless, cut into bite sized cubes
- 1 medium onion, sliced
- 1 can (15.5 ounce) white hominy, drained
- 1 can (14.5 ounce) enchilada sauce
- 3 cups water
- ½ tablespoon canola oil
- ¼ cup green chilies, sliced
- 2 cloves garlic, minced
- ¼ teaspoon cayenne pepper or to taste
- 1 teaspoon dried oregano
- Salt to taste
- 2 tablespoons fresh cilantro, chopped

Directions:
1. Switch on the Instant Pot.
2. Select the "Sauté" function. Press the "Adjust" button once.
3. Add oil. When oil is heated, add pork loin roast and cook until brown.
4. Pour enchilada sauce over it. Spread hominy, onions, garlic, cayenne pepper and oregano over it.
5. Pour water into the inner pot.
6. Close the lid. Select the "Meat/Stew" function and use the default time of 35 minutes.
7. Perform a quick release then enjoy.

Mushroom & Spinach Pasta

Servings: 8
Total time taken: 50 min

Ingredients:
- ¾ pound penne pasta
- 1 ½ pounds smoked sausage, sliced
- 3 cups fresh spinach, sliced
- 4 cloves garlic, minced
- 1 onion, chopped
- 2 cups mushrooms, sliced
- 3 cups chicken stock
- ¾ pound penne pasta
- 1 ½ jars (10 ounces each) roasted red peppers, with its liquid
- ¾ cup parmesan cheese
- 3 cups Monterey Jack cheese

Directions:
1. Switch on the Instant Pot.
2. Add all of the ingredients except cheese.
3. Close the lid. Select the "Meat/Stew" function and "Adjust" up to 45 minutes.
4. Perform a quick release. Add cheese, stir and serve.

Pork Chop Casserole

Servings: 8
Total time taken: 30 min

Ingredients:
- 8 pork chops (1 inch each)
- 2 onions, halved, thinly sliced
- 8 medium potatoes, peeled, rinsed, thinly sliced
- 2 carrots, peeled, thinly sliced
- 2 bay leaves, finely crushed
- 1 ½ cups white wine
- ½ cup chicken stock
- 1 teaspoon garlic powder
- 2 tablespoons parsley, chopped
- ¼ teaspoon red pepper flakes
- 2 tablespoons olive oil
- Salt and pepper
- Pepper powder to taste

Directions:
1. Switch on the Instant Pot.
2. Sprinkle salt and pepper over the pork chops.
3. Select the "Sauté" function. Press the "Adjust" button once. Add oil and pork to the cooking pot in batches and sauté for a while until the pork is brown. Set aside.
4. Pour chicken broth to the pot. Scrape off any brown bits that are stuck to the bottom of the cooker. Press the "Cancel" button.
5. Add half the onions, carrots potatoes to the pot. Sprinkle, salt, pepper, garlic powder, red chili flakes and parsley.
6. Place the pork over the potato layer. Sprinkle the crushed bay leaves over it.
7. Place the remaining potatoes, carrots, and onions over the pork. Sprinkle salt, pepper, garlic powder and parsley over it.
8. Pour wine on top.
9. Cover the lid and select the "Meat/Stew" function and "Adjust" the timer down to 20 minutes.

Pork & Mushrooms

Servings: 3
Total time taken: 4 hrs. 15 min

Ingredients:
- 1 pound country style pork ribs, boneless
- 2 ounce mushrooms, sliced
- ½ a can cream of mushroom soup
- ½ envelope mushroom gravy mix
- A pinch pepper powder
- Salt to taste
- ¼ teaspoon paprika
- 1 tablespoon flour mixed with 2 tablespoons water

Directions:
1. Switch on the Instant Pot.
2. Add all the ingredients except cornstarch.
3. Close the lid. Select the "Slow Cook" function and use the default timer of 4 hours.
4. Add flour mixture and simmer until thick using the "Sauté" function.

Garlic Butter Leg of Lamb

Servings: 2
Total time taken: 4 hrs. 10 minutes

Ingredients:
- 1 leg of lamb that can fit into the crock pot, cut into pieces if desired
- 4 tablespoons butter, chopped
- Salt and pepper to taste
- 2 tablespoons garlic, minced

Directions:
1. Switch on the Instant Pot.
2. Season lamb with salt and pepper.
3. Add the lamb to the inner pot. Sprinkle garlic all over. Place butter at different places on the lamb.
4. Close the lid. Select the "Slow Cook" function and use the default time of 4 hours.

Lamb with Vegetables

Servings: 3
Total time taken: 55 min

Ingredients:
- 3 lamb chops
- 1 large onion, chopped
- 1 medium sweet potato, chopped
- 1 medium potato, chopped
- 1 medium carrot, chopped
- 1 bay leaf
- 2 cloves garlic, chopped
- 1 pod cardamom
- ½ teaspoon turmeric powder
- 1 teaspoon cayenne pepper
- 1 teaspoon ground cumin
- 1 stick cinnamon
- 1 cup broth

Directions:
1. Switch on the Instant Pot.
2. Add all the ingredients into the inner pot then close the lid.
3. Select the "Meat/Stew" function and "Adjust" the timer up to 45 minutes.
4. Perform a quick release then serve and enjoy.

Ground Lamb & Chickpeas

Servings: 6
Total time taken: 45 min

Ingredients:
- 1 ½ pounds ground lamb
- 2 cups carrots, shredded
- 1 ½ cans chickpeas
- 1 pound fresh spinach
- 3 tablespoons curry powder
- 1 teaspoon ground turmeric
- 1 ½ cups chicken broth
- 3 tablespoons lemon juice
- 1 cup almonds
- ¼ cup Greek yogurt
- Salt to taste

Directions:
1. Switch on the Instant Pot.
2. Select the "Sauté" function. Press the "Adjust button once.
3. Add lamb and cook until brown. Add chickpeas, broth and carrots and sauté for 4 minutes. Press the "Cancel" button.
4. Close the lid. Select the Manual option and set the timer for 25 minutes.
5. Add spinach and lemon juice.
6. Cover the lid. Select the "Steam" function and use the default time of 10 minutes.
7. Perform a quick release then add almonds and stir.
8. Serve with a spoon of yogurt on top.

Chapter 11

Instant Pot Fish and Seafood Recipes

Mahi Mahi with Asparagus, Broccoli and Spinach

Servings: 8
Total time taken: 1 hr. 15 min

Ingredients
- 8 mahi mahi fish
- Seasoning of your choice
- 1 tablespoon olive oil
- 2 tablespoons lemon juice
- 1 head broccoli, chopped into florets
- 2 asparagus, chopped into 1 inch pieces
- 1 pound spinach, chopped
- 2 tablespoons water

Directions
1. Switch on the Instant Pot.
2. Mix together in a bowl, seasoning, lemon juice, and oil. Rub it all over the fish.
3. Add all the ingredients into the inner pot.
4. Cover the lid. Select the "Slow Cook" function and set the timer for 1 hour.
5. Serve and enjoy.

Thai Green Fish Curry

Servings: 8
Total time taken: 3 hr. 30 minutes

Ingredients:
- 2 pounds firm white fish, chopped into cubes
- 1 large onion, chopped
- 2 green chilies, deseeded, finely chopped
- 4 tablespoons Thai green curry paste or add according to your taste
- 4 tablespoons sunflower oil
- 4 cm piece fresh ginger or galangal, peeled, finely chopped
- 2 tablespoons fish sauce
- Juice of 2 lemons
- 3 cups coconut milk
- 2 cups vegetable stock
- 6 spring onions, thinly sliced,
- 6 carrots, peeled, chopped into bite sized pieces
- 2 sprigs Thai basil leaves, finely chopped
- Salt to taste
- Pepper powder to taste
- A large pinch ground nutmeg
- 1 cup fresh cilantro leaves, chopped

Directions:
1. Switch on the Instant Pot.
2. Add all ingredients except the spring onions, cilantro, and Thai basil leaves into the inner pot. Stir well.
3. Close the lid. Select the "Slow Cook" function and set the timer for 3 hours.
4. Just before serving, add spring onions, cilantro and Thai basil leaves. Stir well and serve immediately.

Lemon Pepper Tilapia with Asparagus

Servings: 8
Total time taken: 3 hrs.

Ingredients:
- 8 tilapia fillets, thawed if frozen
- 1 bundle asparagus, chopped
- 2 teaspoons lemon pepper seasoning or to taste
- 4 tablespoons butter
- 1 cup lemon juice

Directions:
1. Take 8 foils. Lay the fillets in the middle of the foil. Sprinkle lemon pepper seasoning over it.
2. Place ½ tablespoon of butter on each of the fillets. Place asparagus over the fish.
3. Wrap foil all around the fish. Seal it well.
4. Place the packets in the cooking pot. It can be overlapped while placing it.
5. Switch on the Instant Pot
6. Close the lid. Select the "Slow Cook" function and set the timer for 2 hours if thawed and 3 hours if frozen.
7. Serve and enjoy.

Crawfish Tails

Servings: 8
Total time taken: 30 min

Ingredients:
- 3 cups rice, rinsed
- 2 pounds crawfish tails, peeled
- 2 cans (10.75 ounces each) diced tomatoes with green chilies
- 29 ounces chicken broth
- 1 onion, chopped
- 6 green onions, chopped
- 2 green bell pepper, chopped
- 2 tablespoons dried parsley
- ½ cup butter
- 2 teaspoons Cajun seasoning
- Salt to taste

Directions:
1. Switch on the Instant Pot.
2. Add all the ingredients to the cooking pot and stir.
3. Select the "Rice" function.
4. When complete, perform a quick release then fluff the rice with a fork.

Spicy Lemon Salmon

Servings: 6
Total time taken: 7 min

Ingredients:
- 6 salmon fillets
- 3 tablespoons nanami togarashi
- Juice of 2 lemons
- 1 lemon, thinly sliced
- Salt and pepper to taste

Directions:
1. Switch on the Instant Pot.
2. Pour 1 cup of water into the inner pot. Place the steamer basket in. Mix together all the ingredients and place over the basket.
3. Cover and select the "Manual" option and set the timer for 5 minutes.
4. Perform a quick release. Serve and enjoy.

Mediterranean Tuna Noodles

Servings: 4
Total time taken: 30 minutes

Ingredients:
- 1 ½ cans tuna fish in water, drained
- 1 onion, chopped
- 4 teaspoons olive oil
- 1 ½ cans (14 ounces each) diced tomatoes with basil, garlic, and oregano with its liquid
- Salt and pepper to taste
- 2 cups water
- 12 ounces dry, wide egg noodles
- 1 ½ jars marinated artichoke hearts, drain most of the liquid, chopped
- ½ cup feta, crumbled
- Chopped parsley to garnish

Directions:
1. Switch on the Instant Pot.
2. Select the "Sauté" function. Add onion and sauté until translucent.
3. Add noodles, tomatoes, water, salt and pepper.
4. Close lid. Select the "Soup" function and "Adjust" the timer down to 20 minutes.
5. Perform a quick release.
6. Add tuna and artichokes with retained liquid.
7. Select the "Sauté" function again. Press the "Adjust" button twice. Simmer for 4 minutes.
8. Garnish with feta and parsley.

Scalloped Potatoes with Salmon

Servings: 4-5
Total time taken: 1 hour

Ingredients:
- 10 medium potatoes, peeled, rinsed, sliced
- 2 cans (10 ¾ ounces each) cream of mushroom soup
- 6 tablespoons flour
- 1 cup onions, chopped
- ½ cup water
- Salt to taste
- Pepper powder to taste
- ¼ teaspoon ground nutmeg

Directions:
1. Switch on the Instant Pot.
2. Spray the inside of the inner pot with cooking spray.
3. Lay 1/3 the potato slices in the pot. Sprinkle 1/3 the flour. Season with salt and pepper. Lay 1/3 the salmon and 1/3 the onions.
4. Repeat the above layer twice.
5. Mix together soup and water in a bowl and pour over the layers. Sprinkle nutmeg.
6. Cover the lid. Select the "Meat/Stew" function and "Adjust" up to 45 minutes.
7. Perform a quick release.
8. Serve and enjoy.

Tuna Casserole

Servings: 6
Total time taken: 1 hour 15 minutes

Ingredients:
- 4 cans (7 ounces each) tuna, drained
- 4 cans cream of celery soup
- 2 packages frozen peas, thawed
- 2/3 cup chicken broth
- 1/3 cup buttered bread crumbs or crumbled potato chips
- 1 1/3 cups milk
- 20 ounces egg noodles, cook according to the instructions on the package
- 4 tablespoons dried parsley flakes
- Salt and pepper to taste

Directions:
1. Switch on the Instant Pot.
2. Spray the inside of the inner pot with cooking spray.
3. Add soup, broth, milk, parsley flakes, peas and tuna to the crock-pot. Stir well.
4. Add noodles and fold gently.
5. Sprinkle breadcrumbs.
6. Close the lid. Select the "Multi-grain" function and "Adjust" the timer up to 60 minutes.
7. Perform a quick release.
8. Serve and enjoy.

Fish with Orange and Ginger Sauce

Servings: 6
Total time taken: 15 min

Ingredients:
- 6 fish fillets, pat dried
- 6 spring onions, sliced
- Juice of 2 oranges
- Zest of 1 orange, grated
- 3 tablespoons ginger, minced
- 2 tablespoons olive oil
- 1 ½ cups fish stock or white wine
- Salt and pepper to taste

Directions:
1. Switch on the Instant Pot.
2. Rub fish with olive oil. Sprinkle salt and pepper.
3. Add the rest of the ingredients to the Instant Pot.
4. Place a steamer basket inside the pot. Place fish in the basket.
5. Close the lid. Select the "Steam" function and use the default time of 10 minutes.
6. Perform a quick release.
7. Place fish over a bed of salad greens. Pour sauce over it and serve.

Citrus Fish

Servings: 6
Total time taken: 1 hr. 45 min

Ingredients:
- 2 pounds fish fillets
- 1 large onion, chopped
- 3 teaspoons orange zest, grated
- 3 teaspoons lemon zest, grated
- 1/3 cup fresh parsley, chopped + extra for garnishing
- Salt and pepper to taste
- 2 tablespoons vegetable oil
- 1 orange, thinly sliced
- 1 lemon, thinly sliced

Directions:
1. Switch on the Instant Pot.
2. Spray the inside of the inner pot with cooking spray. Sprinkle salt and pepper over the fish fillets and place in the pot.
3. Sprinkle onions, parsley, orange zest, lemon zest and oil over it.
4. Close the lid. Select the "Slow Cook" function and set the timer for 1-½ hours.
5. Sprinkle parsley. Place orange and lemon slices on top and serve.

Salmon Al Cartoccio

Servings: 6
Total time taken: 2 hrs. 15 min

Ingredients:
- 6 salmon fillets
- 2 medium onions, sliced
- 5 potatoes, thinly sliced
- 6 sprigs each of thyme and parsley
- Salt and pepper to taste
- 1 tablespoon olive oil
- 1 lemon, thinly sliced

Directions:
1. Take 6 foils. Lay the fillets and all the other ingredients in the middle of the foil. Wrap foil all around the fish. Seal it well.
2. Pour 2 cups of water in the inner pot. Place a steamer basket in it.
3. Place the packets on the basket.
4. Close the lid. Select the "Slow Cook" function and set the timer for 2 hours.

Octopus and Potatoes

Servings: 6
Total time taken: 40 min

Ingredients:
- 2 pounds octopus, cleaned, rinsed
- 1 bay leaf
- 1 ½ pounds potatoes, rinsed
- 1 teaspoon whole pepper corns
- Salt and pepper to taste
- 1/3 cup vinegar
- 2 tablespoons parsley, chopped
- 4 tablespoons olive oil

Directions:
1. Switch on the Instant Pot.
2. Place whole potatoes in the inner pot. Add water to just cover the potatoes.
3. Cover the lid. Select the "Steam" function and use the default time of 10 minutes.
4. Perform a quick release then remove the potatoes with a slotted spoon. Don't pour out the water.
5. Place the octopus in the pot. Add pepper, bay leaf, 2 cloves garlic and salt. Add just enough water to submerge the octopus.
6. Cover lid. Select the "Meat/Stew" function and "Adjust" down to 20 minutes.
7. Perform a quick release. Drain the water. Chop the octopus into pieces.
8. Whisk together oil, vinegar, garlic, salt and pepper and set aside.
9. Peel and cube potatoes. Add octopus and the oil mixture. Toss well. Garnish with parsley and serve.

Shrimp Fried Rice

Servings: 2
Total time taken: 30 min

Ingredients:
- 1 cup brown rice, rinsed
- ½ cup onions, chopped
- 1 egg
- 6 ounces frozen shrimp, peeled, deveined
- 2 cloves garlic, minced
- ½ cup frozen peas
- 1 carrot, sliced
- 3 teaspoons sesame oil
- 2 tablespoons soy sauce
- ¼ teaspoon ground ginger
- Salt to taste
- Pepper to taste
-

Directions:
1. Select the "Sauté" function. Add 1-teaspoon of oil. Add egg to the pot and scramble it. Remove on to a plate
2. Add onions and garlic. Sauté until translucent.
3. Add the rest of the ingredients and mix.
4. Cover and select the "Rice" function.
5. When done, add scrambled egg, mix and serve.

Coconut Cilantro Curry Shrimp

Servings: 5
Total time taken: 35 min

Ingredients:
- 1 ½ pounds shrimp, with shells
- ¾ cup Thai red curry sauce
- 5 cups light coconut milk
- 1/3 cup cilantro, chopped
- 4 teaspoons lemon garlic seasoning

Directions:
1. Switch on the Instant Pot.
2. Add all the ingredients into the inner pot. Stir well.
3. Cover the lid. Select the "Bean/Chili" function and use the default time of 30 minutes.
4. Perform a quick release. Add cilantro and stir.

Shrimp and Artichoke Barley Risotto

Servings: 6
Total time taken: 3 hrs.

Ingredients:
- 1 ½ cups onions, chopped
- 1 tablespoon olive oil
- 1 ½ packages (9 ounce each) frozen artichoke hearts, thawed, quartered
- 4 ½ cups boiling water
- 2 tablespoons Better that Bouillon Lobster Base
- 5 cloves garlic, mined
- 1 ½ cups pearl barley
- 1 ½ pounds shrimp, peeled deveined
- 7 ounce baby spinach
- ½ cup parmesan cheese, grated
- 3 teaspoon lemon zest, grated
- Freshly ground black pepper to taste
- Salt to taste

Directions:
1. Add lobster base to boiling water. Whisk well, set aside.
2. Switch on the Instant Pot.
3. Select the "Sauté" function. Add oil and onions and sauté until translucent.
4. Add garlic and sauté until fragrant.
5. Add lobster base solution and rest of the ingredients except spinach, lemon zest, cheese, and shrimp.
6. Close the lid. Select the "Meat/Stew" function and "Adjust" the timer up to 45 minutes.
7. Perform a quick release. Add shrimp and cheese and stir.
8. Close the lid again. Select the "Steam" function and "Adjust" the timer up to 15 minutes.
9. Perform a quick release again. Add lemon zest and baby spinach. Mix well and serve.

Cheese and Prawns

Servings: 2
Total time taken: 20 min

Ingredients:
- 4 shallots, finely chopped
- 1 ¼ cups apple cider or light beer
- 2 tablespoons butter
- 12 ounces raw prawns, peeled, rinsed, pat dried
- 4 teaspoons corn starch
- 2 ½ cups Swiss cheese, grated
- 2 cloves garlic, peeled thinly sliced
- ½ teaspoon hot pepper sauce
- Salt to taste
- French bread or pretzel to serve
- A handful of fresh parsley to garnish

Directions:
1. Mix together in a bowl, cornstarch, apple cider and hot pepper sauce. Pour this mixture into the instant pot and stir.
2. Switch on the Instant Pot.
3. Grease the inside of the pot with a little butter.
4. Add all the ingredients except the parsley into the inner pot. Stir well.
5. Close the lid and select the "Meat/Stew" function and use the default time of 35 minutes.
6. Perform a quick release. Sprinkle parsley on top.
7. Serve with French bread or pretzels.

Seafood Alfredo

Servings: 4
Total time taken: 2-3 hrs.

Ingredients:
- 1 ½ pounds frozen cooked shrimp or seafood blend
- 3 cups milk
- ¼ cup butter
- 1 cup parmesan, shredded
- 1 cup mozzarella, shredded
- 2 teaspoons Herbes de Provence
- Salt and pepper to taste
- 6 cloves garlic, smashed, chopped
- 3 tablespoons flour
- Cooked pasta to serve

Directions:
1. Add milk, flour, garlic, herbs, butter and cheese into the Instant Pot. Mix well.
2. Add the rest of the ingredients except the cooked pasta to the inner pot. Stir well.
3. Close the lid. Select the "Slow Cook" function and set the timer for 2-3 hours.
4. Add pasta, mix well and serve.

Garlic Shrimp & Vegetables

Servings: 6-8
Total time taken: 15 min

Ingredients:
- 4 teaspoons extra virgin olive oil
- 2 large red bell peppers, cubed
- 2 pounds asparagus, trimmed, chopped into 1 inch pieces
- 2 teaspoons lemon zest, grated
- ½ teaspoon salt or to taste
- 6 cloves garlic, finely minced
- 1 pound shrimps, peeled, deveined
- 1 cup low sodium chicken broth
- 1 teaspoon cornstarch
- 2 tablespoons lemon juice
- 2 tablespoons parsley, chopped

Directions:
1. Switch on the Instant Pot.
2. Add all the ingredients into the inner pot. Mix well.
3. Select the "Meat/Stew" function and "Adjust" the timer up to 45 minutes.
4. Perform a quick release then serve and enjoy.

Slow Cooked Crab

Servings: 4
Total time taken: 2 hrs. 15 minutes

Ingredients:
- ¾ pound crab meat, picked, flaked
- 3 tablespoons butter
- 1 can cream of mushroom soup
- 2 tablespoons dry sherry
- ¼ cup light cream
- ½ teaspoon Worcestershire sauce
- Salt to taste
- Pepper powder to taste
- 1 egg, beaten
- 2 green onions, finely chopped

Directions:
1. Switch on the Instant Pot.
2. Add all the ingredients to the inner pot and stir.
3. Close the lid. Select the "Slow Cook" function and set the timer for 2 hours
4. Serve and enjoy.

Shrimp Arrabbiata

Servings: 5
Total time taken: 1 hour 15 minutes

Ingredients:
- 2 pounds frozen shrimp
- 2 onions, chopped
- 1 red bell pepper, chopped
- 1 green bell pepper, chopped
- 12 ounce spaghetti, cooked
- ½ teaspoon crushed red pepper
- 2 teaspoons dried oregano
- 2 teaspoons dried basil
- 2 cans tomato puree
- 6 cloves garlic, minced
- Salt to taste

Directions:
1. Switch on the Instant Pot.
2. Add the shrimp, onions, bell peppers, crushed pepper, oregano, basil, garlic, and tomato puree to the inner pot.
3. Stir and close the lid. Select the "Meat/Stew" function and use the default time of 45 minutes.
4. Perform a quick release. Add spaghetti. Mix well and serve.

CHAPTER 12

Instant Pot Vegetarian Recipes

Enchilada Quinoa

Servings: 4
Total time taken: 2 hrs. 15 min

Ingredients:
- ½ a 15 ounce can black beans, drained, rinsed
- 1 can (15 ounce) mild or medium red enchilada sauce, divided
- ½ a 15 ounce can yellow corn, drained, rinsed
- ½ a 15 ounce can diced fire roasted tomatoes with green chilies
- ½ cup quinoa, uncooked
- ¼ cup water
- 2 ounces Mexican cheese, shredded
- 2 tablespoons fresh cilantro, chopped
- 2 tablespoons sour cream
- 2 tomatoes, chopped
- 1 avocado, peeled, pitted, sliced

Directions:
1. Switch on the Instant Pot.
2. Add all the beans, corn, ½ can enchilada sauce, fire roasted tomatoes, quinoa, water and half the cheese to the cooking pot. Mix well.
3. Pour the remaining enchilada sauce on top. Sprinkle the remaining cheese.
4. Close the lid. Select the "Cook Option" and set the timer for 2 hours.
5. Serve hot.

Golden Squash, Pepper, and Tomato Gratin

Servings: 2
Total time taken: 1 hr. 15 minutes

Ingredients:
- 1 golden squash or yellow squash, chopped
- 1 red bell pepper
- 1 green bell pepper
- 1 onion, chopped
- 1 ½ tablespoons olive oil
- 1 clove garlic, minced
- ½ pound tomatoes, sliced
- 2 tablespoons fresh basil leaves, finely chopped
- ½ cup parmesan cheese
- Salt to taste
- Pepper powder to taste

Directions:
1. Switch on the Instant Pot.
2. Add all the ingredients except the tomatoes into the inner pot. Mix well.
3. Close the lid. Select the "Slow Cook" function and set the timer for 1 hour.
4. Lay the tomato slices over the squash.
5. Serve and enjoy.

Swiss Chard with Chickpeas and Couscous

Servings: 6
Total time taken: 1 hour

Ingredients:
- 2 boxes (10 ounce each) couscous
- 3 cups boiling water
- 4 bunches Swiss chard, trimmed
- 2 cans (15.5 ounce each) chickpeas, rinsed, drained
- 1 cup raisins
- 1 cup pine nuts, toasted
- 4 cloves garlic, sliced
- 1/3 cup olive oil
- Salt to taste
- Pepper powder to taste

Directions:
1. Transfer the couscous into a large bowl. Pour hot water and mix well. Fluff with a fork. Cover and it set aside.
2. Switch on the Instant Pot.
3. Select Sauté option. Add oil and garlic and sauté until fragrant.
4. Add the rest of the ingredients except pine nuts.
5. Close the lid. Select the "Multi-grain" function and use the default time of 40 minutes.
6. Divide the couscous into individual plates. Place the cooked chard and garnish with pine nuts and serve.

Vegetable Curry with Tofu

Servings: 4
Total time taken: 20 min

Ingredients:
- 2 small egg plants, chopped
- 1 large onion, chopped
- 24 ounces extra firm tofu, drained, pressed of excess moisture
- ½ cup frozen peas
- 1 green bell pepper, sliced
- 1 red bell pepper, sliced
- 2 teaspoons fresh ginger, minced
- 2 - 3 tablespoons Thai green or red curry paste
- 1 cup coconut milk
- ½ tablespoon coconut sugar
- ¾ cup vegetable broth
- ¼ teaspoon turmeric powder
- Salt to taste

Directions:
1. To press tofu, place something heavy over the tofu for at least 30 minutes and after that place on paper towels. Finally chop it into bite-sized pieces.
2. Switch on the Instant Pot.
3. Add all the ingredients to the cooking pot and mix well.
4. Close the lid. Select the "Steam" function and "Adjust" the timer up to 15 minutes.
5. Let the steam release naturally for 8 minutes.
6. When done, serve over hot cooked brown rice.

Vegetable Succotash

Servings: 6-8
Total time taken: 15 min

Ingredients:
- 3 cups zucchini, diced
- 3 cups corn kernels
- 1 cup onion, diced
- 2 cups okra, sliced
- 6 cloves garlic, minced
- 4 tablespoons lemon juice
- 2 cans (10 ounces each) seasoned diced tomatoes in juice
- Salt and pepper to taste
- 1 cup vegetable broth
- 1 teaspoon hot sauce
- ½ teaspoon red pepper flakes
- 2 tablespoons fresh parsley, chopped

Directions:
1. Switch on the Instant Pot.
2. Add tomatoes with juice and broth to the inner pot.
3. Add corn, okra, zucchini, onions, garlic, salt, pepper and red pepper flakes and mix well.
4. Close the lid. Select the "Steam" function and use the default time of 10 minutes. Quick release the pressure when complete.
5. Add parsley, lemon juice and hot sauce and mix well.
6. Serve hot as it is or over rice.

Mixed Vegetable Curry

Servings: 2
Total time taken: 20 min

Ingredients:
- 2 carrots, medium sized, sliced
- 1 potato, cut into ½ inch cubes
- 6 fresh baby corns, sliced diagonally
- ½ a 15 ounces can chick peas, drained, rinsed
- 4 ounces fresh beans, stringed, cut into 1 inch pieces
- ½ cup onion, coarsely chopped
- 2 cloves garlic, minced
- 1 tablespoon quick cooking tapioca
- 2 teaspoons curry powder
- ¼ teaspoon red chili flakes
- Salt to taste
- ½ teaspoon coriander, powdered
- 1 big pinch cinnamon powder
- 1 cup vegetable broth
- 1 cup thick coconut milk
- ½ a 15 ounces can tomatoes with its liquid, chopped

Directions:
1. Switch on the Instant Pot.
2. Add the vegetables, chickpeas, tapioca, garlic, and coriander, chili flakes, salt and cinnamon.
3. Pour the vegetable broth over it.
4. Close the lid. Select the "Steam" function and use the default time of 10 minutes. Let the steam release naturally.
5. Add the tomatoes along with the liquid and coconut milk. Stir well.
6. Keep covered for 5 minutes.
7. Serve over hot rice.

Multi-Grain Fried Rice

Servings: 3-4
Total time taken: 45 minutes

Ingredients:
- 1 ½ cups multi-grain rice
- ½ cup carrots, grated
- 2 scallions, sliced
- ½ cup tofu, diced
- ½ cup soy chunks
- 1 ½ cups water
- 1 tablespoon soy sauce
- 1 tablespoon olive oil
- Salt to taste
- ½ teaspoon red chili flakes

Directions:
1. Soak the soy chunks in a bowl of warm water for 15-20 minutes. Squeeze and set aside.
2. Switch on the Instant Pot.
3. Add all the ingredients to the cooking pot and stir.
4. Close the lid. Select the "Multi-grain" function and use the default time of 40 minutes.
5. When the cycle completes, perform a quick release.
6. Fluff rice with a fork and serve.

Fresh Vegetable Mélange

Servings: 2
Total time taken: 15 min

Ingredients:
- 1 large onion, chopped into big pieces
- 2 tomatoes, chopped
- 1 clove garlic, chopped
- 4 new potatoes, sliced
- 1 zucchini, cubed
- 1 large carrot, sliced
- 2 stalks celery, sliced
- 1 small bell pepper, sliced
- ½ cup vegetable broth
- 2 tablespoons fresh dill, chopped
- 2 tablespoons parsley, chopped
- ½ cup frozen peas
- Salt and pepper to taste

Directions:
1. Switch on the Instant Pot.
2. Set the "Sauté" function. Add oil, onions, bell pepper, celery and garlic and sauté until tender.
3. Add the rest of the ingredients.
4. Close the lid. Select the "Steam" function and use the default time of 10 minutes.
5. Perform a quick release then drain extra liquid and serve.

Peas Risotto

Servings: 2
Total time taken: 30 min

Ingredients:
- 1 cup Arborio rice
- 1 medium onion, chopped
- 1 cup frozen peas
- 2 cups vegetable broth
- 4 tablespoons parmesan cheese
- 2 tablespoons butter + extra to serve
- Salt and to taste
- Pepper to taste

Directions:
1. Switch on the Instant Pot.
2. Select the "Sauté" function. Add butter to inner pot then add onions and sauté until translucent.
3. Add broth and peas then stir well.
4. Close the lid. Select the Rice function. When the rice cycle is complete, add, salt, pepper, extra butter and cheese. Mix well and serve.

Lentils with Vegetables

Servings: 4
Total time taken: 25 min

Ingredients:
- 1 cup split green lentils, rinsed
- 2 cups spinach, chopped
- 2 medium carrot, chopped
- 2 cups cabbage, shredded
- 1 onion, chopped
- 6 cloves garlic, sliced
- 1 tablespoon ghee
- 1 ½ teaspoons salt
- 1 teaspoon whole cumin
- ½ teaspoon chili powder
- 6 whole cloves

Directions:
1. Switch on the Instant Pot.
2. Select the "Sauté" function. Add ghee. When the ghee melts, add cloves, and cumin. When cumin crackles, add onion and garlic and sauté until light brown.
3. Add rest of the ingredients and water to cover the ingredients by around 1-½ inches.
4. Close the lid. Select the "Steam" function and "Adjust" the timer up to 15 minutes then let the pressure release naturally.
5. Serve over rice with a sprinkle of lemon.

Vegetable Biryani

Servings: 4-6
Total time taken: 50 min

Ingredients:
- 2 cups basmati rice
- 2 tablespoons biryani masala
- ½ cup peas
- 1 large carrots, chopped
- 2 potatoes, cubed
- ½ cup beans, chopped
- 1 green bell pepper, chopped
- 1 red bell pepper, chopped
- 2 large onions, sliced
- 2 teaspoons ginger garlic paste
- 1 cup yogurt
- 1 teaspoon salt
- ½ teaspoon chili powder
- ½ cup mint leaves, chopped
- 2 tablespoons oil
- ¼ cup cashew, chopped, toasted

Directions:
1. Switch on the Instant Pot.
2. Select the "Sauté" function. Add oil and onions and sauté until brown. Set aside half the onions.
3. Add ginger garlic paste and sauté until fragrant. Add vegetables, yogurt, and biryani masala and cook until almost dry.
4. Add rice, water and salt then stir well.
5. Close the lid. Select the "Rice" function.
6. When the rice cycle is complete, let the pressure release naturally for 10 minutes.
7. Fluff with fork. Add mint leaves, cashew and onions that was set aside. Stir and serve with yogurt.

Vegetarian Conjee

Servings: 2-3
Total time taken: 45 min

Ingredients:
- ½ cup short grain rice
- 1 inch pieces ginger, sliced
- 1 teaspoon sautéed garlic
- 3 dried shiitake mushrooms, soaked in hot water, chopped
- 1 ½ cups water
- 3 cups vegetable broth
- ½ small head bok choy, chopped
- 1 medium carrot, finely chopped
- 2 tablespoons scallions
- Salt to taste
- 2 tablespoons cashews or pumpkin seeds, toasted
- 1 green onion, sliced

Directions:
1. Switch on the Instant Pot.
2. Place rice, mushrooms, stock, water, ginger, carrot, and salt into the inner pot.
3. Stir and close the lid. Select the "Steam" function and "Adjust" the timer up to 15 minutes. Let the steam release naturally.
4. Add bok choy and stir.
5. Select the "Sauté" function. Press the Adjust button twice. Simmer for 10 minutes.
6. Top with garlic and scallions and serve.

Asian Crunchy Noodle Salad Bowl

Servings: 6
Total time taken: 20 min

Ingredients:
- 1 ½ pounds thin spaghetti
- 1 ½ cups bean sprouts
- 1 ½ pounds sugar snap peas, trim ends
- 4 scallions, sliced
- 1 red bell pepper, thinly sliced
- 1 green bell pepper, thinly sliced

Sauce:
- 1/3 cup rice wine vinegar
- 1/3 cup vegetable oil
- ½ cup soy sauce
- 1 ½ tablespoons honey
- 1 ¼ cups crunchy peanut butter
- 5 tablespoons sesame oil
- 3 teaspoons fresh ginger, grated
- 3 cloves garlic, grated
- 5 tablespoons roasted peanuts to garnish
- Cilantro leaves to garnish
- Salt to taste

Directions:
1. Switch on the Instant Pot.
2. Add spaghetti and 6 cups of water into the inner pot.
3. Close the lid. Select the "Steam" function and "Adjust" the timer down to 3 minutes. Quick release the pressure.
4. Rinse and place in a bowl.
5. Add the rest of the ingredients into the Instant Pot and ¼ cup water. Select the "Steam" function and "Adjust" the timer down to 3 minutes again.
6. Perform a quick release, then add to the noodles.
7. Whisk together the sauce ingredients in a bowl and pour over the noodles. Toss well, garnish with peanuts and cilantro and serve.

Vegan Veggie Crumbs Casserole

Servings: 4-5
Total time taken: 2 hrs. 10 minutes

Ingredients:
- 1 cup onions
- 1 cup onions, chopped
- 6 ounces mushrooms, sliced
- 1 cup celery, chopped
- 6 cups dried cornbread or whole wheat bread crumbs
- ½ teaspoon dried thyme
- ½ teaspoon poultry seasoning
- ¾ teaspoon sage
- ¼ teaspoon marjoram
- 2 cups vegetable broth
- Salt to taste

Directions:
1. Switch on the Instant Pot.
2. Add all the ingredients to the inner pot and stir well.
3. Close the lid. Select the "Slow Cook" function and set the timer for 2 hours.
4. Serve and enjoy.

Spinach & Corn Au Gratin

Servings: 4
Total time taken: 1 hr. 20 min

Ingredients:
- 1 ½ cups frozen corn
- 1 pound spinach, thinly sliced
- 2 teaspoons garlic, minced
- 1 ½ tablespoons cornstarch
- ¼ cup flour
- 3 cups cold milk
- 2 tablespoons butter
- ½ cup cheese, grated or more if you like it cheesy
- Salt, red chili flakes, oregano, and pepper to taste

Directions:
1. Switch on the Instant Pot.
2. Select the "Sauté" function. Add butter. When it melts, add garlic and sauté until fragrant and then add flour and cornstarch and sauté for 30 seconds.
3. Add cold milk while whisking simultaneously.
4. Press the Adjust button twice. Simmer until thick. Add salt and pepper and whisk again until it is free from lumps.
5. Add the rest of the ingredients and stir for 5 minutes then press the "Cancel" button.
6. Close the lid. Select the "Slow Cook" function and set the timer for 1 hour.

Vegetable Lasagna

Servings: 4
Total time taken: 30 minutes

Ingredients:
- 1 jar (24 ounce) Italian tomato sauce
- 5 -6 thick lasagna noodles, broken
- 1 large green bell pepper, chopped
- 1 large red bell pepper, chopped
- 2 large carrots, chopped
- 1 cup frozen corn, thawed
- 1 medium zucchini, thinly sliced
- 12 ounce part skim ricotta cheese
- 1 cup Mozzarella cheese, shredded
- ½ cup parmesan cheese, shredded
- 2 tablespoons fresh parsley
- Salt to taste

Directions:
1. Switch on the Instant Pot.
2. Spray the inner pot with cooking spray.
3. Spread about ½ cup of tomato sauce at the bottom of the pot.
4. Lay about 1/3 of the lasagna pieces over it.
5. Make layers by spreading about 1/3 of each of the following; vegetables, salt, sauce, ricotta cheese, mozzarella cheese and lasagna.
6. Repeat the above step twice.
7. Finally spread a thin layer of sauce and top with Parmesan cheese.
8. Close the lid. Select the "Multi-grain" function and "Adjust" down to 20 minutes.
9. Let a natural release occur for 10 minutes.
10. Sprinkle parsley over it. Slice and serve.

Broccoli and Rice Casserole

Servings: 2
Total time taken: 1 hour

Ingredients:
- ¾ cup brown rice, uncooked
- 1 ¼ cup water
- 1 cup mushrooms, finely chopped
- ½ pound broccoli florets, finely chopped
- 1 tablespoon butter
- 2 tablespoons onions, finely chopped
- 1 clove garlic, minced
- 1 cup milk
- 1 tablespoon flour
- ¼ cup walnuts, chopped
- ½ cup low fat cheddar cheese, divided
- 2 tablespoons parmesan cheese, grated
- Salt to taste
- Pepper powder to taste

Directions:
1. Switch on the Instant Pot.
2. Add all the ingredients except the walnuts into the inner pot.
3. Close the lid. Select the "Multi-grain" function and use the default time of 40 minutes.
4. Let a natural release occur for 15 minutes.
5. Garnish with walnuts and serve.

Paneer Tikka Masala

Servings: 8-10
Total time taken: 3 hrs. 15 minutes

Ingredients:
- 2 pounds paneer (Indian fresh cheese) cut into bite size pieces
- 2 large onions, finely chopped
- 1 large onion, chopped into 1 inch squares, separate the layers of the onions
- 1 green bell pepper, chopped into 1 inch squares
- 2 large tomatoes, chopped into 1 inch squares
- 2 tablespoons olive oil
- 6-7 cloves garlic, minced
- 2 inch piece ginger, peeled, grated
- 4 tablespoons tomato paste
- 1 tablespoon paprika or to taste
- 3 teaspoons kosher salt or to taste
- 2 tablespoons garam masala (Indian spice powder)
- 1 ½ cans (28 ounce each) diced tomatoes
- 2 cups coconut milk
- Fresh cilantro to garnish

Directions:
1. Switch on the Instant Pot.
2. Add all the ingredients except cilantro leaves and stir well.
3. Close the lid. Select the "Slow Cook" function and set the timer for 3 hours.
4. Garnish with cilantro leaves and serve hot with naan bread or with rice.

Enchilada Orzo

Servings: 6
Total time taken: 30 min

Ingredients:
- 1 ½ cans (14.5 ounces each) fire roasted diced tomatoes
- 1 ½ cans (4.5 ounces each) chopped green chilies, drained
- 1 ½ cans (10 ounces each) enchilada sauce
- 1 ½ cups canned black beans
- 1 ½ cups corn
- 2 cups vegetable broth
- 3 cups orzo pasta
- 6 ounces cream cheese, cubed
- Salt to taste
- Pepper powder to taste
- 4 tablespoons fresh cilantro, chopped

Directions:
1. Switch on the Instant Pot.
2. Add tomatoes, enchilada sauce, green chilies, broth, corn, salt, pepper and black beans to the inner pot and stir. Place the cream cheese cubes all over.
3. Close the lid. Select the "Manual" option and set the timer for 5 minutes. Let the steam release naturally for 5 minutes. Perform a quick release.
4. Stir and add orzo. Stir again.
5. Close the lid. Select the "Sauté" function. Press the "Adjust" button twice. Cover and cook for 15 minutes.
6. Sprinkle cilantro and serve.

Tofu Salad

Servings: 4
Total time taken: 40 min

Ingredients:
- 1 ½ cups dried chickpeas, rinsed, soaked in water overnight, drained
- 1 cup cooked elbow pasta
- 1 cup frozen corn, thawed
- 1 large tomato, chopped
- 1 apple, chopped
- 1 cup tofu, chopped
- 1 green bell pepper, chopped
- Salt to taste

For the dressing:

- 3 tablespoons apple cider vinegar
- 2 tablespoons honey
- Salt to taste
- Pepper powder to taste
- ½ teaspoon red chili flakes
- 1 clove garlic, minced
- 1 teaspoon dried oregano

Directions:
1. Switch on the Instant Pot.
2. Add the chickpeas and salt to the inner pot. Add enough water to cover the chickpeas (2 inches above the chick peas).
3. Close the lid. Select the "Bean/Chili" function and "Adjust" the timer down to 25 minutes. Let the steam release naturally.
4. Drain and transfer into a large bowl and cool.
5. Meanwhile, whisk together all the ingredients of the dressing in a bowl and set aside.
6. Add the rest of the ingredients. Pour dressing on top and toss well.

Shepherd's Pie

Servings: 6-8
Total time taken: 1 hr. 40 min

Ingredients:
For mashed potatoes layer:

- 1 ½ pounds Yukon gold potatoes, thoroughly washed, halved
- 2 tablespoons butter
- Salt to taste
- Pepper powder to taste

For the lentil layer:

- ¾ cup green lentils, rinsed, soaked in water for 5-6 hours, drained
- 2 cups vegetable stock
- 1 onion, chopped
- 1 clove garlic, minced
- 5 ounce bag mixed frozen vegetables
- ½ teaspoon dried thyme
- ½ tablespoon olive oil

Directions:
1. Switch on the Instant Pot.
2. Add potatoes to the inner pot. Add salt and cover with water. Select the "Congee/Porridge" function and "Adjust" the timer down to 15 minutes. Let the pressure release naturally then drain well and transfer into a bowl.
3. Mash with a potato masher until smooth. Add butter, salt and pepper. Partially cover and keep aside.
4. Select the "Sauté" function. Add oil, onions and garlic and sauté until light golden brown.
5. Add green lentils, vegetable stock, frozen vegetables, and thyme. Press the "Cancel" button.
6. Close the lid. Select the "Manual" function and set the timer for 15 minutes. Perform a quick release.
7. Layer with the mashed potato layer.
8. Cover the lid and select the "Slow Cook" function and set the timer for 1 hour.
9. Serve and enjoy.

Spinach Tortillas

Servings: 4
Total time taken: 2 hrs.

Ingredients:
- ½ a 15 ounce can black beans, rinsed
- 5 ounce frozen spinach, chopped, thawed, squeeze the excess liquid
- ½ cup frozen corn kernels
- ½ teaspoon cumin powder
- 1 cup low fat sharp cheddar cheese, shredded
- Kosher salt to taste
- Black pepper powder to taste
- 1 ½ cup salsa
- 4 tortillas (8 inch), warmed
- 3 cups romaine lettuce, chopped
- 2 radishes, cut into matchsticks
- ¼ cup grape tomatoes, halved
- A few slices cucumber, halved
- 1 ½ tablespoon fresh lemon juice
- 1 tablespoon olive oil
- 1 scallion, sliced

Directions:
1. Mash half the beans in a bowl. Add spinach, corn, cumin powder, and 1/2-cup cheddar, remaining beans, salt and pepper. Mix well.
2. Divide this mixture among the 4 tortillas and roll it up.
3. Spread half the salsa at the bottom of the cooking pot. With the seam side down, place it in the pot in a single layer. Pour the remaining salsa over it. Sprinkle the cheddar over it.
4. Switch on the Instant Pot.
5. Close the lid. Select the "Multi-grain" function and use the default time of 40 minutes.
6. Let the pressure release naturally for 15 minutes. Before serving, mix together lettuce, radish, tomatoes, and cucumber. Add lemon juice, oil and salt and pepper.
7. Serve with hot tortillas topped with scallions.

Creamy Mushroom Polenta

Servings: 6
Total time taken: 25 min

Ingredients:
- 2 cups polenta
- 2 tablespoons olive oil
- 1 ½ pounds mushrooms, sliced
- 1 onion, chopped
- Salt and pepper to taste
- 8 cups vegetable stock
- 4 tablespoons butter
- 2/3 cup cheese, grated

Directions:
1. Switch on the Instant Pot.
2. Add all the ingredients into the inner pot.
3. Close the lid. Select the "Multi-grain" function and "Adjust" down to 20 minutes.
4. Perform a quick release then stir and serve.

Daal Maakhni

Servings: 6
Total time taken: 45 min

Ingredients:
- 1 cup black lentils, soaked in water overnight, drained
- ½ cup kidney beans, soaked in water overnight, drained
- 1 cup tomato puree
- 1 tablespoon ginger paste
- 1 tablespoon garlic paste
- 1 tablespoon ghee
- 1 teaspoon whole cumin
- 1 teaspoon chili powder
- 2 teaspoons salt
- 1 tablespoon butter
- ½ cup cream

Directions:
1. Switch on the Instant Pot.
2. Add all the ingredients into the inner pot and stir well. Pour enough water to cover about 2 ½ inches above the ingredients.
3. Select the "Bean/Chili" function and "Adjust" up to 45 minutes.
4. Let the pressure release naturally for 15 minutes.
5. Serve with naan bread or over rice.

Vegetarian Tacos

Servings: 6-8
Total time taken: 35 min

Ingredients:
- 1 cup Portobello mushrooms, sliced
- 2 stalks celery, finely chopped
- 1 green chili chopped or more if you like is spicy
- 1 medium onion, finely chopped
- 1 medium green bell pepper, chopped
- 1 clove garlic, minced
- ¼ cup tomato puree
- ½ cup vegetable stock
- ½ tablespoon olive oil
- 2 teaspoons taco seasoning
- 1 can (15 ounces) kidney beans, rinsed, drained
- Salt to taste
- Pepper to taste
- 6-8 readymade taco shells
- ¼ cup plain yogurt
- 1 tablespoon cilantro, chopped
- ½ cup cheese, shredded

Directions:
1. Switch on the Instant Pot.
2. Add all the ingredients except tacos shells into the inner pot and stir well.
3. Select the "Bean/Chili" function and use the default time of 30 minutes.
4. Perform a quick release.
5. To fill the tacos: Spoon in about 2-3 tablespoons of the filling into each of the taco shells. Sprinkle cheese and cilantro. Top with about a teaspoon of yogurt and serve.

Chapter 13

Instant pot Dessert Recipes

Peanut Butter Chocolate Cheesecake

Servings: 4
Total time taken: 25 min + chilling time

Ingredients:
- 3 eggs
- 24 ounces cream cheese, softened
- 2 tablespoons cocoa
- 3 tablespoons powdered peanut butter
- ¾ cup swerve sugar substitute
- 1 ½ teaspoons vanilla extract
- Whipped cream and peanut butter to top

Directions:
1. Switch on the Instant Pot.
2. Add all the ingredients into a blender and blend until smooth. Divide and transfer into 4 mason jars. Cover with lid or foil.
3. Pour 2 cups of water into the pot. Place a trivet in the pot.
4. Place the jars on the trivet inside the pot. Cook in batches if required.
5. Close the lid. Select the "Steam" function and "Adjust" the timer up to 15 minutes.
6. Let the steam release naturally then chill for a couple of hours and serve.

Mini Salted Caramel Mocha Cheesecakes

Servings: 8
Total time taken: 2 hrs. + Chilling time

Ingredients:
For mocha cheesecakes:

- 1 ½ cups ground chocolate graham crackers or chocolate wafers
- 2 large eggs
- ½ cup butter, melted
- 16 ounces cream cheese, softened
- 2/3 cup sugar
- 1 teaspoon instant coffee
- 2 ounces bittersweet chocolate, melted, slightly cooled
- ¼ teaspoon salt
- 1 teaspoon vanilla extract

For salted caramel:
- 2 cups packed brown sugar
- 2 tablespoons vanilla extract
- 8 tablespoons unsalted butter
- 1 cup heavy whipping cream
- Whipped cream for serving
- 1 teaspoon salt

Directions:
1. Switch on the Instant Pot.
2. Spray 8 canning jars of 4 ounces each with cooking spray.
3. Mix together in a bowl crackers and butter. Divide and add to the jars. Press lightly.
4. Add sugar and cream cheese to a large bowl and beat until smooth.
5. Add eggs, chocolate, vanilla, coffee and salt and beat again. Pour into the jars (up to ¾).
6. Place the jars in the Instant Pot. Pour warm water all around the jars. The jars should be covered up to ¾ with water. Cook in batches if needed
7. Close the lid. Select the "Slow cook" function and set the timer for 1-½ hours.
8. Perform a quick release then chill for a couple of hours.
9. Meanwhile, make the salted caramel as follows: Place a heavy bottomed saucepan over medium heat. Add butter, brown sugar, cream and salt. Stir constantly and cook until well blended.
10. Add vanilla and simmer for a minute. Remove from heat and cool.
11. Spoon salted caramel over the cheesecake. Top with whipped cream and serve.

Chocolate Fudge

Servings: 6
Total time taken: 1 hr. + chilling

Ingredients:
- 1 ¼ cups dark chocolate chips
- ¼ cup coconut milk
- 2 tablespoons coconut sugar or honey or maple syrup
- A pinch of sea salt
- 1 tablespoon coconut oil
- ½ teaspoon vanilla extract
- 2 tablespoons walnuts, chopped into small pieces

Directions:
1. Switch on the Instant Pot.
2. Add all the ingredients to the inner pot. Mix well.
3. Close the lid. Select the "Slow Cook" function and set the timer for 1 hour.
4. Let it cool to room temperature. Now stir constantly for a few minutes.
5. Transfer the mixture into a greased tin. Cover and refrigerate until the fudge is set. Chop and serve.

Cherry Dump Cake

Servings: 6
Total time taken: 1 hour

Ingredients:
- ½ yellow cake mix
- ¼ cup butter, melted
- 1 can (21 ounces) cherry pie filling

Directions:
1. Switch on the Instant Pot.
2. Mix together cake mix and butter in a bowl.
3. Pour the cherries into a greased inner pot. Pour batter over it.
4. Close the lid. Select the "Multi-grain" function and use the default time of 40 minutes.
5. Let the pressure release naturally for 15 minutes.
6. Uncover, cool for a while.
7. Slice and serve. Tastes great with vanilla ice cream.

Mango Coconut Rice Pudding

Servings: 8-10
Total time taken: 15 min

Ingredients:
- 2 cups Arborio rice
- 2 cans light coconut milk
- 2/3 cup brown sugar
- 3 cups water
- 1 cup half and half
- ¼ teaspoon salt
- 2 ripe mangoes, peeled, cubed
- 2 teaspoons vanilla
- ½ cup almonds, chopped + extra to garnish
- ½ cup shredded coconut

Directions:
1. Switch on the Instant Pot.
2. Add rice, water, coconut milk, brown sugar and salt to the cooking pot. Stir.
3. Close the lid. Select the "Manual" option and set the timer for 8 minutes.
4. Perform a quick release then add rest of the ingredients and stir. Chill if desired
5. Spoon into bowls. Garnish with almonds and serve.

Strawberry Pudding

Servings: 8
Total time taken: 1 hr. 20 min

Ingredients:
- 2 cups plain flour
- 2 eggs, beaten
- 3 teaspoons baking powder
- 1 pound strawberries, chopped into small pieces
- 5 tablespoons dried breadcrumbs
- 1 cup butter, chopped
- 1 cup granulated sugar
- 10 ounces milk
- 1 teaspoon salt
- Whipped cream to serve

Directions:
1. Mix together the dry ingredients in a bowl. Add butter and mix. Add milk and eggs and beat well. Add strawberries and stir. Transfer into a greased baking tin.
2. Place a trivet inside the inner pot. Pour 2 cups of water. Place the dish over the trivet.
3. Close the lid. Select the "Multi-grain" function and "Adjust" the timer up to 60 minutes.
4. Quick release the pressure then serve and enjoy. Chill if desired.

Chocolate Peppermint Pudding

Servings: 6-8
Total time taken: 45 min

Ingredients:
For cake:
- 1 ½ cups all purpose flour
- 6 tablespoons cocoa
- 9 ounces melted dark chocolate
- 1 ½ tablespoons baking powder
- 3 eggs
- ½ teaspoon salt
- 1 ¼ cups brown sugar
- ¾ cup heavy cream
- ¾ cup butter at room temperature
- 1 ½ teaspoons vanilla
- 1 ½ teaspoons peppermint candy, finely ground + extra for topping

For glaze:
- 1 ½ cup chocolate chips, semi-sweet
- ¾ cup heavy cream

Directions:
1. Switch on the Instant Pot.
2. Beat butter and sugar in a bowl until sugar dissolves. Add an egg at a time and a little flour at a time and mix until well combined.
3. Add rest of the ingredients and mix into a smooth batter.
4. Grease a pan and pour the batter into it. Cover with foil.
5. Pour 2 cups of water in the inner pot and place a trivet in it. Place the pan over it.
6. Close the lid. Select the "Multi-grain" function and "Adjust" the timer down to 20 minutes.
7. When done, perform a quick release then remove the pan from the pot. Discard water.
8. For glaze: Add cream to the Instant Pot. Select the "Sauté" function and bring to a boil. Switch off the pot and add chocolate chips. Stir until it melts.
9. When the pudding is completely cooled, invert on to a plate. Pour glaze over the pudding. Sprinkle peppermint candy powder over it
10. Slice and serve.

Mixed Berry Pudding

Servings: 6
Total time taken: 1 hr. 15 minutes min

Ingredients:
- ¼ pound red currants, halved
- ¼ pound raspberries
- ¼ pound strawberries, chopped
- ¼ pound plums, pitted, chopped
- 1 ½ cups water
- ¼ cup corn starch
- ½ cup red wine
- Milk or cream to serve

Directions:
1. Switch on the Instant Pot.
2. Set aside a cup of berries, and add the rest to the inner pot. Add sugar and stir.
3. Cover the lid. Select the "Slow Cook" function and set the timer for 1 hour.
4. Mix together in a bowl, cornstarch, and water and pour into the pot.
5. Select the "Sauté" function. Stir constantly until it thickens. Press the "Cancel" button.
6. Add the red wine and mix well.
7. Blend the berries that were set aside and add to the thickened berries.
8. Can be served either hot or cold. Serve with milk or cream.

Pumpkin Custard

Servings: 4
Total time taken: 45 minutes + chilling time

Ingredients:
- 1 cup cooked pumpkin
- 3 eggs
- 2 tablespoons full fat coconut milk
- 2 tablespoons maple syrup or honey or 1 packet stevia
- ¼ teaspoon ginger
- 1 teaspoon pumpkin pie spice
- A pinch salt

Directions:
1. Switch on the Instant Pot
2. Pour water into the inner pot to cover at least an inch from the bottom.
3. Blend together all the ingredients. Grease ovenproof ramekins and pour the blended mixture into the ramekins. Keep it 2/3 full.
4. Carefully place the ramekins in the pot.
5. Cover the lid. Select the "Multi-grain" function and use the default time of 40 minutes.
6. Let the pressure release naturally for 15 minutes then serve and enjoy.

Spiced Apple Crunch

Servings: 8-10
Total time taken: 30 min

Ingredients:
- 6 apples, cored, sliced
- 2 cups dry bread crumbs
- ½ cup butter, melted
- Zest of 2 lemons
- Juice of 2 lemons
- 1 teaspoon ground cinnamon
- 1/8 teaspoon ground nutmeg
- ½ cup sugar
- 2 cups water

Directions:
1. Grease a baking dish with butter.
2. Mix together in a bowl, breadcrumbs, sugar, cinnamon, lemon juice and zest.
3. Place a single layer of apples in the dish. Sprinkle some of the mixture over it. Repeat this step until all the apples and the mixture is used up.
4. Drizzle butter all over. Cover with foil.
5. Switch on the Instant Pot.
6. Pour water in the inner pot and place a trivet in it. Place the dish over it.
7. Close the lid. Select the "Steam" function and "Adjust" the timer up to 15 minutes. Let the steam release naturally.
8. Serve warm and enjoy.

French Orange Crème

Servings: 12
Total time taken: 20 minutes + chilling

Ingredients:
- 9 yolks
- 1 ½ cups milk
- 1 cup sugar
- 1 ½ cups cream
- 1 teaspoon orange zest
- Blackberries to garnish
- Blackberry syrup to top

Directions:
1. Pour milk and cream into a saucepan and place it over medium heat. Remove from heat when it just begins to bubble and cool.
2. Whisk together yolks and sugar until sugar dissolves.
3. Add orange zest. Pour milk mixture into this and whisk until well combined.
4. Pour into ramekins and cover each ramekin with foil.
5. Switch on the Instant Pot.
6. Pour 1 ½ cups water into the inner pot. Place a steamer rack in it.
7. Place the ramekins over it.
8. Close the lid. Select the "Steam" function and use the default time of 10 minutes.
9. Perform a quick release then remove ramekins. Uncover, cool and chill.
10. Garnish blackberries and blackberry syrup over it and serve.

Flan with Caramelized Almonds

Servings: 12
Total time taken: 45 min + chilling time

Ingredients:
Flans:
- ½ cup agave syrup,
- 3 cups low-fat milk
- 2 fresh vanilla beans, or 2 tablespoons vanilla extract
- 6 extra-large eggs
- 4 egg yolks
- 1 cup firmly packed dark brown sugar

Caramelized walnuts:
- 2/3 cup almonds, chopped
- 2 tablespoons agave syrup
- 2 tablespoons brown sugar

Directions:
1. Flans: Put 2 teaspoons of agave syrup at the bottom of 12-15 individual small ovenproof serving bowls. Place the bowls in the refrigerator for at least 15 minutes.
2. Meanwhile, place a saucepan over medium heat. Add milk and the black paste of the vanilla beans (scrape with a knife) and the pods. When the milk is hot, remove from heat. Keep aside for 10 minutes.
3. In a large bowl, add eggs, yolks, and brown sugar. Whisk well.
4. Slowly pour 1 cup of the heated milk into the bowl. Whisk constantly. Repeat with the remaining milk.
5. Pour the custard back to the pan after sieving.
6. Pour the custard into the small serving bowls.
7. Switch on the Instant Pot.
8. Place a steamer rack or basket inside the inner pot. Pour 2 cups of water.
9. Place dish over the rack.
10. Close the lid. Select the "Manual" option and set the timer for 25 minutes. Let steam release naturally. Chill.
11. To serve, run a knife around the edges and invert on to a plate. Top each flan with a tablespoon of caramelized almonds

12. Meanwhile caramelize the almonds as follows: Grease a baking tray and place the almonds on it. Pour agave syrup and brown sugar. Mix well to coat thoroughly.
13. Bake at 300 degree F for 8-10 minutes or until done.
14. Remove from oven and place on a wax sheet to cool.

Crème Brulee

Servings: 6 -8
Total time taken: 15 min

Ingredients:
- 6 egg yolks
- ¼ cup granulated sugar
- 1 teaspoon vanilla extract
- ¼ cup granulated sugar
- 4 tablespoons very fine sugar
- A pinch of salt
- 1 ½ cups heavy cream

Directions:
1. Whisk together in a bowl, yolks, sugar, and salt. Add cream and vanilla and whisk until well blended.
2. Strain the entire mixture into a pitcher. Pour this mixture into 4 - 5 custard cups or ramekins. Cover each of the cups with aluminum foil.
3. Switch on the instant pot.
4. Place a trivet at the bottom of the inner pot. Pour about 1-½ cups of water.
5. Place the cups on the trivet.
6. Close the lid. Select the "Manual" option and set the timer for 6 minutes. Let the pressure release naturally.
7. Open the lid.
8. Remove the cups after a while. Uncover and cool.
9. Serve warm or chilled. Serve sprinkled with fine sugar. Hold a kitchen torch 3-4 inches away from the custard. Heat with the torch and caramelize the sugar by moving the flame of the kitchen torch in a circular manner until light brown.

Else you can broil for a few minutes until golden brown.

Caramel Custard

Servings: 6
Total time taken: 45 min + chilling time.

Ingredients:
- 2 cups milk
- 4 eggs, beaten
- ½ cup + 8 tablespoons white sugar
- 2 tablespoons water
- 2 tablespoons hot water or as required
- 1 teaspoon vanilla extract

Directions:
1. Place a heavy saucepan over medium heat. Add ½ cup sugar and 2 tablespoons water and heat until it begins to boil.
2. Lower heat slightly and cook without stirring until golden brown syrup is formed.
3. Remove from heat and let it cool for a minute. Add hot water and stir. Pour into a baking dish or divide and pour a little into each ramekin or custard cups. Let it cool. It will harden.
4. Meanwhile, place a saucepan over low heat. Add 8 tablespoons sugar and milk. Stir constantly until sugar is dissolved and milk is lukewarm.
5. Remove from heat and add eggs and vanilla extract. Whisk well. Pour the egg mixture over the caramel set dish or ramekins.
6. Switch on the Instant Pot.
7. Place a trivet inside the inner pot. Pour 2 cups of water.
8. Place the dish over the trivet.
9. Close the lid. Select the "Multi-grain" function and "Adjust" down to 20 minutes.
10. Allow 15 minutes for a natural release then chill.
11. To serve, run a knife all around the edges of the pan and invert on to a plate.
12. Sprinkle nutmeg and confectioners' sugar and serve.

Stuffed Peaches

Servings: 10
Total time taken: 20 min + chilling time

Ingredients:
- 10 peaches
- 4 tablespoons butter, melted
- ½ cup maple sugar
- ½ cup cassava flour
- 2 tablespoons almonds, finely chopped
- 1 teaspoon ground cinnamon
- 1/8 teaspoon salt
- 1 teaspoon almond extract
- 2 cups water

Directions:
1. Slice the top of the peach and discard it. Carefully remove the pits using a knife
2. Mix together butter, flour, cinnamon, ½ teaspoon almond extract and salt.
3. Stuff this mixture into each peach.
4. Switch on the Instant Pot.
5. Pour water and ½ teaspoon almond extract into the instant pot. Place a trivet.
6. Place peaches in a heatproof bowl over the trivet.
7. Close the lid. Select the "Steam" functions and "Adjust" the timer down to 3 minutes.
8. Quick release the pressure.
9. Cool and serve with vanilla ice cream.

Apricot Crisp

Servings: 6
Total time taken: 2 hrs. 10 min

Ingredients:
- 1 can (20 ounces) apricots, drained, sliced
- ½ cup packed light brown sugar
- 1/3 cup ground crackers
- 2 tablespoons butter, unsalted, divided

Directions:
1. Switch on the Instant Pot.
2. Grease the inside of the inner pot with cooking spray.
3. Layer with half the apricot slices followed by half the cracker crumbs followed by brown sugar and finally half the butter.
4. Repeat the above layer.
5. Close the lid. Select the "Slow Cook" function and set the timer for 2 hours.
6. Serve warm.

Chocolate Covered Pretzel Rods

Servings: 4 - 6
Total time taken: 1 hr. 10 min

Ingredients:
- 15 ounces pretzel rods
- 1 ½ cups baking chocolate chips
- Toppings of your choice like chopped nuts or sprinkles

Directions:
1. Switch on the Instant Pot.
2. Fill the inner pot with water up to around 1/3. Place the chocolate chips in jars.
3. Place the jars in the pot gently so that no water enters the jars. Do not cover jars.
4. Close the lid. Select the "Slow Cook" function and set the timer for 1 hour. Stir frequently.
5. Gently remove the jars from the pot. Line a baking sheet with parchment paper. Dip each pretzel (up to half) in the melted chocolate. Shake off excess chocolate sprinkle toppings and place in the baking sheet. Set aside for a while to harden and store.

Sugared Walnuts

Servings: 2-3
Total time taken: 2 hrs. 15 minutes

Ingredients:
- 8 ounces walnuts, chop into big pieces (say ¾ inch)
- 2 tablespoons granulated sugar
- 2 tablespoons brown sugar
- 4 tablespoons butter
- ¼ teaspoon ground cloves
- ¼ teaspoons ground allspice
- ½ tablespoon ground cinnamon

Directions:
1. Switch on the Instant Pot.
2. Add all the ingredients to the inner pot and stir.
3. Close the lid. Select the "Slow Cook" function and set the timer for 2 hours. Stir frequently.
4. When done, transfer into and bowl and cool completely.
5. Transfer into an airtight container and store.

Calabash Halwa

Servings: 5 - 6
Total time taken: 35 minutes

Ingredients:

- 4 cups calabash (bottle gourd), peeled, grated
- 1 ½ cups milk
- ½ cup sugar
- 3 tablespoons ghee
- 20 cashew nuts, chop each into 3-4 pieces
- 4 tablespoons raisins
- ½ teaspoon ground cardamom

Directions:

1. Switch on the Instant Pot.
2. Add 1 tablespoon of ghee to the inner pot. Add raisins, sauté until they puff up. Remove and keep aside. Add cashew, sauté until light brown, remove and keep aside.
3. Add the remaining ghee to the pot. Add calabash and sauté for 3-4 minutes. Add milk and stir.
4. Close the lid. Set the "Steam" function and use the default time of 10 minutes.
5. Perform a quick release then use the "Sauté" function and simmer until the liquid dries up. Stir on and off.
6. Now add sugar and continue cooking until the sugar is melted and the pudding is thick.
7. Add the cardamom, roasted cashew, and raisins and cook for a few seconds more.
8. Serve hot or warm but not cold.

Blackberry Grunt

Servings: 6-8
Total time taken: 2 hrs. 30 min

Ingredients:
- 7 tablespoons sugar
- 2 cups blackberries, fresh or frozen
- 1 teaspoon almond extract
- ¼ cup water

For dumplings:
- 1 tablespoon butter,
- 1 cup all purpose flour
- ½ teaspoon sugar
- 2 teaspoons baking powder
- 14 teaspoon salt
- 6 tablespoons milk

Directions:
1. Switch on the Instant Pot.
2. Add blackberries, sugar, water and vanilla to the inner pot and mix well.
3. Close the lid. Select the "Slow Cook" function and set the timer for 2 hours.
4. Meanwhile make the dumplings as follows: Mix together all the ingredients of the dumpling except milk and mix to get a crumbly texture.
5. Add milk and mix to get soft dough.
6. After 2 hours of cooking, place spoonfuls of dumplings all over the blackberry mixture.
7. Close the lid. Select the "Multi-grain" function and "Adjust" the timer down to 20 minutes.
8. Perform a quick release then serve warm.

Berry Compote

Servings: 12
Total time taken: 20 min

Ingredients:
- 2 cups blueberries, divided
- 2 cups blackberries, sliced
- 2 cups raspberries
- 4 tablespoons lemon juice
- 2 tablespoons water mixed with 2 tablespoons cornstarch
- 1 ½ cups sugar

Directions:
1. Switch on the Instant Pot.
2. Add raspberries, blackberries, sugar, lemon juice and 1/3 of the blueberries into the inner pot. Stir.
3. Close the lid. Select the "Steam" function and "Adjust" the timer down to 3 minutes. Release excess pressure after 10 minutes.
4. Select the "Sauté" function. Add cornstarch mixture and stir constantly until the mixture thickens. Switch off the Instant Pot.
5. Add remaining blueberries and stir.
6. Chill and serve.

Caramel Fondue

Servings: 6
Total time taken: 2 hrs.

Ingredients:
- 12 soft caramels, unwrapped
- 3 tablespoons mini marshmallows
- 3 tablespoons heavy cream or milk
- ¼ teaspoon fine sea salt

Directions:
1. Switch on the Instant Pot.
2. Add caramels, milk, salt, and mini marshmallows to the inner pot.
3. Close the lid. Select the "Manual" option and set the timer for 20 minutes.
4. Perform a quick release then serve with fruits or cookies or pretzels.

Conclusion

I would like to thank you once again for purchasing this book.

By now, you would have realized about how versatile an appliance the Instant Pot is and how it is an efficient cooking appliance. You will simply have to throw in all the required ingredients into it, and then wait for it to do its magic. You can whip up delicious home cooked meals that will lighten up your day. After a long day at work, wouldn't it be nice to come back to a bowl of hot, home-cooked food?

The Instant Pot has not only got different uses but benefits as well. One of the many advantages of cooking in an Instant Pot is that you will be able to cook food in batches and freeze it up for future use. This not only saves time but effort as well. You will be able to cook delicious and nutritious food by making use of the recipes that have been provided in this book. You will simply need to plan ahead and make sure that your pantry is well stocked.

The next time you have your friends or family over for a meal, you can whip up a delicious three-course meal by making use of the recipes given in this book and put your Instant Pot to good use. Make use of the various preset modes and different methods of cooking for making a tasty meal.

Thank you and all the best!

Made in the USA
San Bernardino, CA
06 March 2017